THE AMERICAN NIGHTMARE

Strategies for Preventing, Surviving & Overcoming Foreclosure

By Sylvia Alvarez and Walter Walker Jr.

Published by
S&B Publishing
550 N. Reo Street, Suite 300
Tampa, FL 33509
(813) 872-9323

ISBN 978-0-9817007-0-0

First Printing – May 2008

For all those who pursue the *American Dream* of home ownership.

This book is also dedicated to Marge Calabro, who served tirelessly and faithfully since the early beginnings of the Housing & Education Alliance. Because of her dedication and hard work thousands of families know the joy of home ownership. Marge has gone on to a better place, and we know she is up there making sure everything is run just right. We miss you Marge, and all the baked "goodies" you always brought. You wouldn't be happy with the price of flour down here anyway, and we know we will see you again one day. Till then, we'll carry you in our hearts.

TABLE OF CONTENTS

ACKNOWLEDGEMENTS

The information in this book is drawn from both government and private sector sources. Some of these sources include the Department of Housing and Urban Development / Federal Housing Administration (HUD / FHA), National Association of Hispanic Real Estate Professionals (NAHREP), Department of Veterans Affairs (VA), Department of Labor, FreddieMac, FannieMae, National Council of La Raza (NCLR), First American Title, NeighborWorks America, and many members of the Mortgage Industry-at-large, as well as other industry participants.

We would also like to acknowledge Pat Halpin, Nichole Alvarez-Sowles, Mark Broderick and the HEA staff of Sandra Fernandez-Lopez and Linda Van Doren for their contributions to review and editing.

DISCLAIMER

This book was written to serve as an aid to those who may be facing foreclosure, but it is also a guide to all homeowners. It will show strategies to avoid foreclosure, and if necessary overcome it. Our purpose is not to provide legal advice or recommendations which guarantee a particular outcome. This book is intended to provide information which is available from a variety of sources in a clear concise manner. The reader is *strongly* encouraged to seek out and work with housing and legal professionals who are best equipped to be of assistance to Homeowners in trouble with their mortgages. The information contained in this book is not intended to constitute legal advice or to substitute for obtaining legal advice from an attorney, licensed in the relevant jurisdiction.

The Housing & Education Alliance is a HUD certified housing counseling agency established in 2002 to promote homeownership. Their staff members were awarded the Tampa Housing Authority's **Housing Heroes Award** in July of 2004 and the Tampa Bay Hispanic Chamber of Commerce's **2005 Non-Profit of the Year Award**. In February of 2005 Catholic Charities awarded HEA the **Outstanding Community Services Award**, and in 2007 NeighborWorks America awarded them **the Innovations in Homeownership Contest** for their ***My Home America Housing Expo 2006.***

HEA's mission is to provide and sustain homeownership opportunities through homebuyer education, counseling, lending and development – essentially empowering families and individuals to build wealth through homeownership.

From its inception in 2002 until 2007, HEA has delivered over 260,000 hours of education and one-on-one counseling to over 15,000 families and/or individuals on the subject of financial literacy and the home buying process. Out of those served, approximately 1,500 purchased their first home either with or without government down payment assistance.

INTRODUCTION

YOU ARE NOT ALONE. If you are reading this book you may be like millions of homeowners today who are finding themselves in great financial distress over one of the most prized and sought after possessions most of us will ever own... our homes. This book was written to address the overwhelming need for guidance, answer your many questions, and share information regarding the options you may have. It is our hope you will get some peace of mind and a clearer vision so you can approach this situation armed with the knowledge and information necessary to arrive at the best option for you.

We will point out the reasons people find themselves facing foreclosure and take you through a step-by-step analysis of your situation, the available choices you can make, and their repercussions. You will understand the lender's point of view and learn how to best present your case to them in order to arrive at a favorable outcome for all concerned. This book also contains information regarding resources available to help you navigate through the decision making and negotiating process. Most are free of charge.

Most importantly, we want to let you know you *can* turn things around and start out again on the right foot. Whether you ultimately lose your home, or are able to negotiate with your lender to stay, you can make the right choices. You will learn steps to rebuild your credit and yes, even if you lose your home, you can buy again if you follow the steps we have outlined.

It is our sincere hope that the process outlined in this book will arm you with the knowledge and confidence needed to make the wisest decision for your specific circumstances. We aim to give you the peace of mind that you *do* have options, and that there *is* a way out of this financial dilemma. Most importantly, should you have to leave your home, you *can* rebound - and we will show you how!

The American Nightmare was written to provide a ready reference guide and tool for use by those who are experiencing the pain of impending foreclosure. It is not intended to take the place of professional guidance or the personalized help which may be required. This book may not reflect the most current legal developments and under no circumstances should you rely solely on this material. You should seek independent and competent legal counsel or the help of a HUD certified housing counselor, especially if facing foreclosure or bankruptcy. The information contained in this book is not intended to constitute legal advice or to substitute for obtaining legal advice from an attorney, licensed in the relevant jurisdiction. It is, however, intended to provide a basic understanding of the steps a lender may take in order to legally obtain your property should you fail to make your required mortgage payments or otherwise fail to arrive at some other mutually acceptable solution.

> **"This is *not* the time to lose faith in yourself."**

This information has been gathered from various reliable sources, and gleaned from the combined experience of the authors. We did not set out to provide *all* of the answers to the many perplexing questions surrounding the foreclosure process. That would be nearly impossible. It is our intent to present to you some possible solutions. Please keep in mind, the best way to resolve your current crisis is to learn about and understand your options and what you should be willing to do in order to keep your house.

You must first develop mental toughness. This is not the time to lose faith in yourself. As long as you are able to make rational decisions and have some funds to work with there may be hope for you. Take the advice provided, and most importantly - do not attempt to do this on your own! A note of caution: there are those who have recently become "Local Area Experts" in foreclosure prevention. All too often they are not, and have ulterior motives not in line with your desire to keep your home. As in any crisis, there will be profiteers whose only intent is to make a profit while relieving you of your property. Some of these people will be disguised as "Realtors®" and others as "investors" seeking to buy your home. Please don't misunderstand our meaning. Not all Realtors® or investors are going to tell you that your only choice is to sell your home, or make an effort to steal your house by offering far less than its true value. There ***are*** reputable realtors who can help you through this process!

In the Appendix you will find the "Code of Trust" written by the National Association of Hispanic Real Estate Professionals. This document will provide the reader with insights into the best practices of all who take part in the home buying process - and what you can expect and *demand* from them. It represents what NAHREP members consider to be the "gold" standard for serving their clients, and we hope it becomes the standard for *all* real estate professionals.

This book will also give you a better understanding of the foreclosure process. If there are items you don't understand please ask someone who does know, and if you still don't understand ask again and keep asking until you do. Refer to the *Resource Guide* in the back of the book for places you can seek guidance.

You must not lose heart. This is not the time to be faint of spirit. You must be strong and maintain faith. If you take the appropriate actions and follow instructions, you likely stand a good chance of succeeding in your quest to keep your house. Prepare yourself, as well as your documents, because you may be in for a long and difficult struggle. Gather your family around and have a candid conversation with them, discuss the relevant circumstances of your situation, and talk about what may happen. You must be willing to make some difficult decisions, and if required take what may appear to be drastic measures.

The action(s) you will need to take will depend upon your individual circumstances. You will most likely need to prepare a "crisis budget." Do it as soon as you believe trouble is on the horizon. This may be difficult to foresee, as you will be in the middle of what may be a series of ongoing crisis' - each bigger and more difficult to address than the previous. Stop and assess your situation. This is not the time to be foolish, or to put your head in the sand. Gather your resources, and decide what you have to work with and what you are willing to do - i.e. what actions you and your family are either *capable* of taking or are *willing* to take. Do not make promises you cannot keep, as this will only make the situation worse and possibly ruin a good relationship with a creditor you may need as an ally.

Review your priorities with the entire family, and discuss what you are prepared to live without and how you are going to make ends meet during a difficult time. If you have children, now is the time to have a conversation about giving up frivolous items or activities which cost money. These may be the temporary measures which enable you to keep your home. Your house is your largest single asset, and if you are able to keep it and continue making your monthly payments, even if you have had some difficulties, it may be in your best interest to do so. On the other hand, it may be that you are *not* in a position to keep your house. If that is the case, you must be strong enough to deal with that reality as well.

Our intention is to give you the knowledge required to understand what may happen, and some of the reasons for what may take place. Armed with this knowledge, you can face the uncertainties with a better idea of how you may be successful and what might done to secure your future. The material contained should be used as the tool it was intended to be, and not as the only source of information. Learn from it and use it as a springboard to a better understanding and, hopefully, future success.

One of the keys to success is understanding the steps the mortgage company may take and what options may be available to you, along with what you may be able to ask the lender to do to help work things out. Remember, in the current financial and real estate climate, your lender does *not* want to take your house - but they *will* if you fail to resolve the situation. Due to market conditions, lenders are more inclined than at any other time to work with you and be of assistance in helping you keep your home.

What we are saying is if you are able to survive the crisis, this may be the best time for you to work yourself out of a bad situation. Read the book to get a basic understanding of the material - and then read it again. The second time read it for clarity and understanding. Learn the terms and the options available so you can be in a better position to help yourself. Visit the websites, read the information contained, and discuss your situation with a HUD certified housing counseling agency.

You must learn as much as you can in a very short time, while under a great deal of stress. Prepare yourself for what is to come by listening to those around you who have your best interests in mind. Make an appointment with an experienced counselor affiliated with a HUD certified housing counseling agency and keep it, bring everything you are asked to, and make copies if you are asked. Be willing to listen to your counselor, and resolve to take action as required. This book is intended to give you a point of reference so that when something is said by your counselor, your realtor, or the mortgage company you can better understand what they are talking about and the options being presented. The bottom line is you will be better equipped to make wise decisions rather than poor ones based on incomplete information or emotion.

Take your time and familiarize yourself with your situation. Develop a plan of action - one that you develop on your own after reading the book - and take it to your counselor for review. It is better to have a clear plan with an objective, than a poorly developed plan rushed into action with haste and no forethought.

You will find some content stated and restated several times while reading this book. That is intentional, because it is often best to have certain information conveyed in a variety of ways. When we speak of lenders we may refer to them as lender, mortgage company, or your servicer because these are all terms which refer to the same organization - the people you send your payments to. The authors are confident you will appreciate the manner in which the material is presented, and have taken great pains to make this book as user friendly as possible. We hope you find it both useful and beneficial.

WHAT IS FORECLOSURE?

"Nothing is to be feared, only understood."

- Madame Curie

WHAT IS FORECLOSURE?

Foreclosure is a legal term which can be simply defined as a mortgage holder recalling a debt or accelerating mortgage payment to the entire balance being "due in full" upon notice. This typically happens if the borrower is more than three months behind in payments and has made no effort to bring the mortgage current. A more complete "legal" definition can be found below:

> **Foreclosure:** ***a legal proceeding in which the bank or lender can take possession of and sell a mortgaged property when the borrower does not meet his or her contractual obligations, e.g. is delinquent on payments. Foreclosure remains on your credit report for seven years.***

Mortgage payments are typically due on the first day of each month unless your lender has agreed in writing to a different day. If your payment is not received by the due date, i.e. the first day of the month, your payment is considered to be late - although most loans provide a grace period after which a late charge is applied to your monthly payment. Lenders usually allow for a ten to fifteen day grace period, therefore if your monthly payment is due on the first day of the month with a ten day grace period and is received on the 11th day of the month it is considered late on the second day of the month and a late charge is accessed on the 11th day of the month.

You are classified as *delinquent* when you fail to make one or more monthly mortgage payments. A lender recognizes different degrees of delinquency according to the number of missed payments and the reasons given for the default. You may become delinquent due to an injury, illness, loss of employment or for many other reasons. What the lender looks at is the reason for the delinquency and your desire and ability to pay. Lenders are typically willing to work with you to bring the loan current and are often open to repayment plans. Your lender wants to be certain you can and will make your mortgage payments on time. Remember, your mortgage company isn't in the real estate business. They want your money, not your house, so they are inclined to be of help to you – but they *will* take your house if you fail to make the payments.

THE FORECLOSURE PROCESS

When you fall behind on your loan payments the lender or servicer has the legal right to foreclose on the loan. This means the lender or servicer has the legal right to force you to move out and can sell the property at a public auction to pay off the loan. Foreclosure procedures vary from state to state and are established by state statutes, case law, and local rules.

METHODS OF FORECLOSURE

The two methods of foreclosure are ***judicial foreclosure*** and ***non-judicial foreclosure***. A judicial foreclosure sale is conducted after a court has entered a judgment and order of sale and requires the filing of a lawsuit. A non-judicial foreclosure sale is a private sale conducted under the "power of sale" clause contained in the loan agreement. Some states allow both judicial and non-judicial foreclosure processes, and the decision about whether to foreclose judicially or non-judicially rests with the lender after consultation with their attorneys. Even after the foreclosure process has begun, many states allow you to pay the installments due and any costs of the foreclosure to keep the mortgage. All states allow you to pay the total outstanding debt before the sale, plus costs and interest.

JUDICIAL FORECLOSURE PROCESS

The judicial foreclosure process can be broken down into three main phases: Pre-Foreclosure,

Foreclosure, and Post Foreclosure. There are steps the lender must take prior to filing a foreclosure action, and these steps fall under the pre-foreclosure phase. From the time the foreclosure action is filed until the time the property is sold on the courthouse steps, this is considered 'the foreclosure phase.' What occurs after the Certificate of Title is issued is considered the 'post foreclosure phase.' In the following pages we will discuss each phase in more detail. Again, the information contained in this book is not intended to constitute legal advice or to substitute for obtaining legal advice from an attorney licensed in the relevant jurisdiction. If you are facing foreclosure we strongly recommend you seek guidance from a licensed attorney.

As an overview, the lender or servicer must file an action with the court to receive a judicial decree authorizing the foreclosure sale. The lender or servicer must prove that there is a valid mortgage between the parties (you and the lender); that you, the borrower, are in default of the mortgage; and that the proper procedure has been followed. You have the opportunity to raise procedural and substantive defenses to the foreclosure in addition to filing a counterclaim against the lender.

THE PRE-FORECLOSURE PHASE

- **Breach Letter:** A breach letter may be

required under the terms of the loan or by state law. If it is required, the lender must send a letter or notice to you, the borrower, which provides that a breach has occurred. The breach letter has many different names and may be referred to as a demand letter, notice of intent to foreclose ("NOI"), or notice of default ("NOD"). The claimed breach can either be a monetary breach (such as failure to make a monthly payment) or a non-monetary breach (for example, if you gave a deed on the property to another without paying off the loan and without the consent of the lender). If the breach is a monetary one the breach letter must contain the date of the breach, the amount needed to bring the loan current, and a reasonable amount of time to bring the loan current - usually 30 to 45 days. It should also contain a clause stating failure to pay the amount shown by the due date may result in the lender seeking a legal remedy including the filing of a foreclosure action. The breach letter may be sent out directly from the lender, a specialty company hired by the lender, or an attorney retained by the lender. How a breach letter is to be sent, i.e. first class mail, certified mail, etc., is determined by either the loan documents or state law.

- **Payment accepted and applied after breach letter:** If you were to send in the full amount shown on the breach letter within the time provided the lender will not seek a legal remedy such as foreclosure, however if you sent in less than the amount indicated on the breach letter the lender may accept and apply the insufficient funds to the loan or may instead refuse to accept the insufficient funds and return them to you. Please understand that if the lender accepts the insufficient funds and applies them to the loan they are still due the remaining amount to fully reinstate the loan, although state law may require the lender to send a new breach letter prior to moving forward with filing a foreclosure action. If the lender refused the insufficient funds and returned the funds to you they may proceed directly to filing a foreclosure action once the time to reinstate the loan noted on the breach letter has expired.

- **Filing of bankruptcy *after* the breach letter but *before* a foreclosure action is filed:** For purposes of the pre-foreclosure phase, we will briefly discuss the affects of bankruptcy after the breach letter is sent but before the filing of a foreclosure action. The bankruptcy filing acts as an automatic stay with regard to any actions against you, the debtor, and your property. If after the bankruptcy action the lender was not made whole, in some states the lender is required to send another breach letter prior to proceeding with foreclosure. If the loan was discharged in the bankruptcy action the lender can still file a foreclosure action (an action against the property) but may not seek a judgment against you personally. What this means is after the foreclosure sale, should the lender not recoup the full amount due and owing to them, they cannot seek the remaining amount from you *personally*, by way of a deficiency judgment. We will discuss deficiency judgment in more detail in the post foreclosure phase below.

- **Notice required by the FDCPA:** In addition to the breach letter the lender is required by federal law to provide you, the borrower, with a notice commonly referred to as the "hello letter." This notice may also be called the *validation notice*. The lender is required to send the validation notice to you, the consumer, within five days of the initial communication with you regarding the collection of a debt. The validation notice must contain the amount of the debt, the name of the creditor, and a clause that you have thirty days in which to dispute the validity of the debt - otherwise the debt will be assumed to be valid. If the debt or a portion of the debt is disputed within the thirty day window the lender must provide validation of the debt, mail the validation to the consumer, and include a clause that upon written request of the consumer within the thirty days the debt collector will provide the name and address of the original creditor if different than the current creditor. If you, the consumer, notify the debt collector within the thirty day period that you dispute the debt or that you request the name and address of the original creditor, they must cease all collection activity (that means they cannot file a foreclosure action) until they have provided you with the validation or name and address of the original creditor. In some instances lenders or their debt collectors will include the FDCPA Notice in the Breach Letter.

THE FORECLOSURE PHASE

- **In Rem Action:** The foreclosure action is a

law suit *In Rem.* In Rem is a Latin term meaning "against a thing." In a foreclosure action it means 'against the property.' To explain in more detail, the lender provides you with a loan to purchase a piece of property. The *Note* is the document which provides the terms of the loan. The Note is your personal obligation on the loan. The Mortgage, on the other hand, is the document which outlines the collateral on the loan, that is, the property you purchased with the money you borrowed. When a lender files the foreclosure action they are suing based on the terms of the mortgage, thus they are seeking an action against the property.

- **Lis Pendens:** *Lis Pendens* is a Latin term meaning "pending action." The purpose of the Lis Pendens is to provide notice that there is a pending action against the property. The notice of Lis Pendens should be filed with the complaint and recorded in the property records in the county where the property is located.

- **Complaint:** This is the first document filed with the court and initiates the lawsuit. The Plaintiff in the foreclosure action would be the holder of the note and mortgage (i.e. the lender). There may be many defendants named in the foreclosure action. The first defendant listed will be the title holders to the property. The title holder is typically the borrower of the loan unless the borrower has given a deed to another person after the loan was obtained. Additional defendants named can include the second mortgage lender, Home Owners Associations, Condo Associations, the State, and any other junior lien holders and possibly tenants. Once served with the complaint, you have a limited time to file a response or answer the complaint.

- **Suit on the Note:** A suit on the note is an action against you personally for the full amount due under the terms of the note. Some jurisdictions may allow the lender to pursue a suit on the note at the same time as the foreclosure action. Lenders may also seek a suit against you personally, after the foreclosure action, by way of a deficiency action.

- **Final Judgment:** To obtain judgment the lender must prove their interest is superior to that of the title holder, their lien is superior to the liens and interests of junior lien holders and interest holders, the entire balance of the debt secured by the mortgage held by the Plaintiff is due and collectible, and that they are entitled to collect costs and attorney fees pursuant to the terms of the mortgage. If the judgment is entered, the judgment extinguishes the Defendant's interest in the property and directs the Clerk to sell the property.

- **Notice of Sale:** Is sent out after the judgment is entered. It provides the date, time and location of the foreclosure sale and is required to be published in a newspaper.

- **Bidding Process:** The Plaintiff receives a credit bid at the foreclosure sale in the amount of the judgment plus post judgment interests and costs. The Plaintiff's bid will be the opening bid at the foreclosure sale.

- **Certificate of Title:** The successful bidder at the foreclosure sale will receive a certificate of title after the full amount of the bid is paid to the clerk. There is usually a short period of time between when the bidder's money is paid and the time the Certificate of Title is issued. The Certificate of Title acts like a deed and places the title of the property in the name of the successful bidder.

- **Right of Redemption:** Redemption is your right to pay off the loan in full. Depending on State law, the time to redeem the loan may only be available for a certain period. For instance, you may have until the time of the foreclosure sale to redeem the loan or until the Certificate of Title is issued.

You may have a defense to the foreclosure action or even a counterclaim (lawsuit) against the lender. You also have the right to file discovery requests during the foreclosure action. You may also have other rights such as the right to reinstate the loan during foreclosure or the right to object to the foreclosure sale, therefore, we strongly recommend you seek the advice of a licensed attorney.

THE POST FORECLOSURE PHASE

- **Deficiency Judgment:** A deficiency is the balance of the debt after applying the proceeds from the sale of the property. If the lender does not recover the full amount due from the proceeds of the foreclosure sale, and assuming the debt has not been discharged in a bankruptcy action, the lender may pursue a Deficiency Judgment against you personally to recover the balance due on the loan.

- **Eviction:** Once the final judgment is entered your ownership interest is extinguished. The successful bidder at the foreclosure sale is provided the title to the property through the certificate of title, and you become a 'tenant in possession.' The successful bidder will need to file an eviction action to obtain possession of the property. It is possible to avoid an eviction action if you are able to work out an agreement with the successful bidder regarding a timeframe to move out of the premises on your own.

PHASES OF NON-JUDICIAL FORECLOSURE

Typical non-judicial foreclosures include the following phases:

- The trustees first send you a *Notice of Default and Election to Sell.* Depending on the laws of your state, the court is not directly involved in the process. In non-judicial states, generally speaking, the mortgage company simply begins the foreclosure process without filing a law suit as a result of your being in default.

- **The Reinstatement Period**: Your reinstatement period at this point may be very short and your options may be limited. It is highly recommended that you consult an attorney or at the very least consult a HUD certified housing counselor for advice and recommendations. Do *not* attempt to take care of the situation by yourself - the results could be catastrophic.

- **The Notice of Trustee's Sale:** Official notice is given that the property will be sold on a specific date at a specific location.

- **The Redemption Period:** The period during which a borrower may reclaim the title and possession of property by paying off the entire loan amount. Please note that redemption is *different* from reinstating the loan, which generally refers to bringing the loan current by making the missed mortgage payments.

- **The Trustee's Sale**: A public auction where numerous properties are sold to the highest bidders. This could be your final opportunity to redeem your property by paying the past due balance plus attorney's fees and costs at or prior to the sale.

NON-JUDICIAL OR "POWER OF SALE" FORECLOSURE

In some states the lender or servicer is permitted to sell the mortgaged property at a foreclosure sale without filing a court action. In the non-judicial foreclosure, the lender or servicer obtains a "power of sale" by means of a clause which is included in the mortgage or deed of trust. This clause indicates that in the event of a default in payments or any other breach of the loan terms, the holder of the mortgage may conduct a sale of the property after providing you the notice required by the terms of the mortgage or by applicable statutes.

NON-JUDICIAL ("POWER OF SALE") FORECLOSURE PROCESS

There are many states which use Deeds of Trust rather than mortgages. An example of a non-judicial foreclosure, as applied to California properties, is the following:

- **The Notice of Default (NOD**) starts the non-judicial foreclosure process. The lender forwards a Declaration of Default and an Instruction to the Trustee to proceed with the NOD. The Trustee will sign and record the NOD in the office of the county recorder of public records of the appropriate county, parish or borough etc.

- A copy of the NOD is mailed to all parties (including the borrower) entitled to its receipt. The Trustee will order a Trustee's Sale Guarantee (TSG) from a title company. The TSG discloses the priority of any and all liens recorded against the property and provides the mailing information for the parties entitled to receive the NOD.

- **Three (3) Month Reinstatement Period:** This is the minimum period required by California law that a lender must wait before a Notice of Trustee's Sale can be published and recorded. Throughout the foreclosure process, up until five (5) days prior to the Trustee's Sale date or postponed sale date, the borrower can fully reinstate the loan. In other words the mortgage company is made whole (meaning the past due payments are brought current) and everything is as it was before the foreclosure process began.

  The lender may endeavor to negotiate a workout or forbearance agreement. Depending on the type of mortgage loan you have, whether FHA, VA, or conventional financing, your options will vary from few to many.

- **Notice of Trustee's Sale – the 21 Day Publication Period:** No sooner than three (3) months from the recording date of the NOD, a Notice of Trustee's Sale indicating the place, date and time of the sale must be published in a local newspaper. Twenty-one (21) days thereafter the property may be eligible for public auction to the highest bidder. As stated previously, the borrower has the right to reinstate the loan up until five (5) days prior to the published sale date or postponed sale date. In the event the NOD was filed due to a balloon payment and/or maturity date, the lender(s) may require the loan be paid in full at any time during the foreclosure.

- **The Trustee's Sale:** The Notice of Trustee's Sale will designate the date, time and location of the auction. Hundreds of properties may be scheduled on the same date, and the auctioneer offers the properties for sale individually to the bidders in attendance.

“...at some point... your right to reinstate the loan by making the past due payments may cease!”

CAUTION: Your right to save your home from auction by simply bringing the payments current, as opposed to satisfying the loan, is a matter of state law and/or the loan documents. As a general rule, at some point during the non-judicial foreclosure process your right to reinstate the loan by making the past due payments may cease. When that happens, you may have to pay off the loan entirely (including any costs and attorneys fees incurred by the lender) and such payoff will generally have to occur before or at the auction.

CONSEQUENCES OF FORECLOSURE

If a foreclosure is completed and your house is sold, it is rare that you can do very much to recover the property. In states with redemption periods, you can reclaim the home after the sale date by repaying the entire debt. In states without redemption periods, the property belongs to the mortgage company or the highest bidder immediately after the sale. In rare cases you can question the procedure of the foreclosure and have the right to start legal action against the lender or servicer in order to recover the home. In some instances, you may question the amount of money the lender or servicer is claiming to be owed.

If the property was sold for less than the lender or servicer was owed, you may be responsible for paying the balance due and outstanding property taxes (depending on the state). If the property was sold for more than was owed to the lender or servicer you may receive some money back. The borrower may have to request any surplus funds from the court, and it may vary from state to state. Either way there may be tax consequences to you, as governed by local laws and the IRS. Due to recent changes in the law borrowers will now not have an IRS tax consequence on their homes if the home sells for less than the amount owed. You should contact a tax accountant or attorney to determine if you bear any liability. Another serious consequence of foreclosure is that, after the sale of the home, your credit record will include the foreclosure.

FORECLOSURE FROM THE LENDERS PERSPECTIVE

The lender does not want your house. They want the return on their investment. The lender has an agreement with you which they expect you to fulfill. They have based profit projections on the yield of funds collected from the mortgage. The lender does not want to be in the real estate business - they are in the money lending business. Having said this, remember that they will take your house if you fail to make your mortgage payments. Foreclosure from the lenders perspective is a legal process, and is one they must take in order to preserve their legal rights to the property if you have failed to make your payments. Foreclosure is not a situation the lender is anxious to undertake, as it will take time and cost money which they are not likely to recoup. The lender can lose as much as $40,000 or more on an average foreclosure.

The lender is not in a position to manage property, because they are in the *lending* business. While a home is sitting vacant waiting for sale it is accruing costly insurance premiums, taxes, repairs, and bringing in no return on the lender's investment. The lender is losing even more because of the lost interest they could be receiving on their asset. They have their money invested, but make nothing from that investment until the property sells. If a short sale can be accomplished part of their money is returned and they are no longer losing money. In a short sale the lender may even be willing to finance a new owner, making it a win/win for all parties.

OTHER METHODS OF FORECLOSURE

There are two other less common methods of foreclosure:

- **Strict Foreclosure**: This type of foreclosure is allowed in Connecticut, for example, and possibly other states as well. The lender or servicer must go to court to obtain a court order declaring you to be in default on the mortgage. As a consequence, the title of the property shifts to the lender or servicer. The court sets a time for you to pay the debt and redeem the property. No sale is involved in this foreclosure. Although there is a period of time for you to redeem the property, that time may be short. Time is of the essence!

- **Entry and Possession**: This type of foreclosure is used in Maine, Rhode Island, New Hampshire, and Massachusetts for example. Based on the terms of the mortgage document, the lender or servicer enters onto the property and takes physical possession. This type of foreclosure is used in combination with non-judicial foreclosure by Power of Sale process.

PHASES OF THE FORECLOSURE PROCESS

The length of time the foreclosure process will take, the type of notices the lender or servicer is required to give you, and the actual sale procedures will vary according to the type of foreclosure undertaken and the statutes or laws of each state. Non-judicial and judicial foreclosures involve different phases and actions taken by the lender or servicer.

PRINCIPLE CAUSES OF FORECLOSURE

"Every great mistake has a halfway moment, a split second when it can be recalled and perhaps remedied."

- Pearl S. Buck

Reason for Foreclosure	Percentage
Curtailment of Income	58.3%
Illness/Medical	13.2%
Divorce	8.4%
Investment/Unable to Sell	6.1%
Low Regard for Prop. Ownership	5.5%
Death	3.6%
Payment Adjustment	1.4%
Other	3.5%

Having good money management and financial planning skills may not help you avoid delinquency, because it is not always possible to predict or avoid the financial hardships and crises you may undergo. The information in this section will be of help if you have defaulted on your loan and your home is at risk of foreclosure. You should be at least minimally familiar with some of the remedies available should you encounter any of the problems discussed. Such remedies may include working with a HUD certified counseling agency which may be able to assist with some credit issues or financial advice, all the way to contacting an attorney for the purpose of declaring bankruptcy if that becomes necessary.

Some primary reasons people go into foreclosure:

- Loss of employment
- Loss of income
- Divorce
- Death in the family
- Excessive/costly repairs or maintenance
- Credit card debt
- Adjustable rate mortgages
- Poor understanding of the buying process
- Equity stripping
- Insufficient escrow
- Rising taxes and insurance

Loss of Employment or Income: In most households where there is a dual income both are used to qualify for the mortgage, and the loss of either or a portion of one or both will have a lasting and serious impact on the household budget.

Repairs and Maintenance: Buying a house which was not in proper condition or is in need of greater repairs than the buyer is financially capable of addressing is another reason for mortgage default.

Credit Card Debt: Having too much credit card debt is one of the leading reasons for mortgage default. The availability of easy credit and seemingly endless cash to meet any want or need is very tempting and often leads to problems with mortgage payments. Homeowners all too frequently place themselves in situations where they are in fear of losing their standing among friends and family and end up overextending themselves financially to their own detriment.

Poor Understanding of Home Buying and/or Mortgages: A lack of understanding and education regarding the home buying and mortgage process can be one major source of ongoing difficulty. Not understanding how your mortgage works, or what is required with monthly payments, can lead to foreclosure. There are many different types of mortgages, each with different requirements.

Equity Stripping: *Equity stripping* is one of the many scams which may be presented to home owners in trouble with their mortgages. It is the process of having the "equity" value of your home systematically taken away by refinancing your mortgage. This practice is similar to using your house as an ATM machine. Be careful, beware of all who tell you they are "here to help," and remember the old adage "all that glitters is not gold."

Insufficient Escrows: This means you have an insufficient amount of money in your *escrow* account. Simply stated, there is not enough money to pay for property taxes and insurance premiums which are included in your monthly payment. For example, you bought a house and the taxes were a lot less than they should be and for whatever reason you did not know this – and as a result you did not properly plan for the difference. Many home buyers fail to understand the tax bill of the previous owner is not necessarily *their* tax bill.

Types of Mortgages:

- Fixed rate – 15/30/40 year
- Adjustable Rate Mortgages – ARM
- Negative Amortization Adjustable Rate Mortgages
- Interest only
- Balloon
- Home Equity Mortgage
- Home Equity Line of Credit
- Sub-prime Loans
- Hybrid Loans

Property Taxes and Insurance: These are subject to change and can be especially volatile. The mortgage payment can rise to a point beyond the borrower's ability to pay. Not all states have homestead exemption or circumstances where the property taxes are capped over a period of time. If your taxes are escrowed, they are calculated as a percentage of the home value. Taxes are usually calculated as a percentage of the home's value and the amount is divided into twelve (12) equal installments and added to the monthly mortgage payment. The same may apply to the insurance payment. When property taxes and insurance rates go up they can rise a great deal as compared to where they were upon initial purchase, resulting in an increased monthly mortgage payment.

When escrows for taxes and insurance are not part of the monthly mortgage payment, the homeowner will have to make the total payment when due. This can create a large financial hardship, as the total amount due can be in the thousands of dollars. For example: in Florida taxes are due in November, and insurance is due on the anniversary date of the policy - which is usually the date of closing.

Adjustable Rate Mortgages: ARMs can be another reason people are likely to go into foreclosure. The rate adjusts at a predetermined time, and the homeowner must be aware of this time frame and be ready to make the new mortgage payment when due. The inability to do so when the time comes will in many cases lead to financial distress and/or foreclosure, and not understanding how or when the mortgage payment will adjust and by how much can lead to disaster. It is important for consumers to understand the different types of mortgages (see glossary for definitions):

Negative Amortized Mortgages: These loans can be difficult to understand. Negative amortization, also known as Neg Am, occurs whenever the loan payment you are required to make is less than the actual payment (what the payment *really* is). The difference between these payments is added to the mortgage balance. These loans can vary greatly, can have different features, and are very complex. Negative amortization loans are one of the primary causes of the mortgage foreclosure crisis, and you should **never** consider one.

This is the essential information you need to know. Any or all of these conditions can cause a change in mortgage payment or housing expenses, and several combined together can lead to a very serious condition and cause major distress.

Surviving a Financial Crisis: It is important to understand it is not a good idea to take on additional debt to repay old ones. Instead, if you are experiencing a financial crisis, you should identify and address the cause. You should first determine whether the situation is a temporary financial problem or a long-term difficulty. Making this distinction will help you decide on a strategy for dealing with your circumstance and avoid foreclosure by knowing what happened to cause the situation and what will be the result. Will the situation change, or get worse, and what can you do to have a positive impact?

If you should experience serious financial distress the first thing to do is contact the mortgage company, let them know you are having difficulty, and explain your situation. They will not forgive the lack of a mortgage payment, but this will at least buy you some time to begin developing some type of plan toward a resolution.

WHAT ARE YOUR OPTIONS?

"I gain strength, courage and confidence by every experience in which I must stop and look fear in the face . . ."

- Eleanor Roosevelt

Before you decide if foreclosure, bankruptcy, or other options are right for you it is wise to consult with an attorney or HUD certified housing counseling agency for advice. As housing counselors we simply want to present the options available to you, and highly recommend seeking legal counsel or a consultation with a HUD certified housing counselor before taking any steps. The following options are available:

Credit and Foreclosure Prevention Counseling Resources: Professional credit counseling is a good option when you are facing a financial crisis. The personal and emotional distress caused by the idea of losing your home may lead to anxiety and disorientation. A counseling professional who is trained to objectively analyze financial situations can make useful recommendations and help you gain some perspective in order to deal with your debt more effectively. Ensure that you engage the services of a "true" counseling agency, not one with the objective of relieving you of your money or your house. There are counseling agencies that don't really want, or know how to, be of actual service when you are in need. Ask for a referral from your lender, turn to ***www.HUD.gov***, or call your local Government Housing Office. What you want is an agency which specializes in being of actual assistance to people in need. To find more about HUD approved agencies and their services, call toll free (800) 569-4287 on weekdays between 9:00 a.m. and 5:00 p.m. Eastern Standard Time (6:00 a.m. to 2:00 p.m. Pacific Time). The same number will provide you with an automated referral to the three housing counseling agencies located closest to you. Two types of counseling resources are described below:

- **Credit Counseling:** A credit counselor is a professional trained in credit intervention who can advise you on crisis budgeting, payment plans, and strategies for saving your home.

- **Housing Counselors:** If you're in default on your mortgage loan you may receive counseling assistance from a HUD approved housing counselor in resolving your mortgage problems.

Credit Counseling: There are two types of credit counseling companies: nonprofit, and private. It is highly recommended that you use the services of a true HUD certified or approved *nonprofit* counseling agency. Many private agencies charge a high fee for counseling which you may not be able to afford. In some cases they may actually instruct you to take out another loan, or place the charges on a credit card! The same services can often be obtained from a nonprofit company which charges a smaller fee, or no fee at all. You should be especially wary of 'counseling companies' which ask for large amounts of money up front or monthly fees to work with you. Also be aware that these agencies will generally not be allowed to *represent* you unless they are attorneys. In some instances they only want to take you down the road to bankruptcy, or are looking for a way to take your away house.

"There have been reported cases of credit counselors who have deceived consumers and disappeared with their money."

There are legal means which can be employed by unscrupulous agencies claiming to represent you which allow them to take your house. Generally this would be because you have signed some piece of paper which gives them permission to act on your behalf. You should not give any money to a counselor associated with such a company, and should not allow the counselor to make a payment arrangement on a debt. Your mortgage company may not allow someone to make arrangements in your name. They may speak with and discuss the situation with them, but will not make final arrangements. There have been reported cases of credit counselors who have deceived consumers and simply disappeared with their money. You must be aware of unscrupulous firms looking to take advantage of financial adversities.

There are some non-profit companies which feed for-profits such as mortgage companies. They will ask if you are a homeowner, and will seek to have you re-finance or take out an equity line of credit in order to consolidate your loans. This may be the very reason you are in difficulty. You may have listened to someone who did not have your best interests in mind. What they wanted was to line their pockets, and you paid the price. In actuality they may have no interest in helping resolve your credit issues beyond creating a new line of debt.

There are many credit counseling resources to be found on the internet. Some of them are private companies which describe themselves as working for not-for-profits. Some provide a computerized evaluation which requires you to fill out a form to help identify your financial situation, and subsequently provides for personal or computerized counseling. Attempting to work out a financial problem through a computer can be both beneficial and harmful. While it may seem advantageous to deal with personal problems in an impersonal way from the privacy of your home, it is dangerous to disclose private information to a company or individual over the internet or telephone without first verifying their legitimacy and the security of your personal information. You are also at risk of inadvertently pressing the wrong key on the keyboard or accidentally choosing the wrong feature offered by the computer program, thus receiving an erroneous output. Also remember that even though the site may be "secure," you are still in danger of being a victim of identity theft. There is a growing problem with internet predators stealing other people's identities, so be very careful about how you choose to submit personal information for review. The fastest growing crime in America today is identity theft, so don't place yourself in further jeopardy by being less than vigilant at all times.

See the Resource Guide for a link to HUD's website and access to a current list, or visit ***www.myhomeamerica.com*** for more information on credit counseling agencies in your area.

Housing Counselors: If you're in default on your mortgage loan you may be eligible to receive counseling assistance from a HUD approved housing counselor to help resolve your mortgage mortgage to consult with or seek the services of a HUD approved counseling agency. The U.S. Department of Housing and Urban Development (HUD) has approved several hundred agencies, and provides funds directly or indirectly to many of them for mortgage default counseling. Although these agencies are HUD-approved and in some cases are funded by HUD to deliver FHA mortgage default counseling, many of them will also provide assistance if you have a VA or conventional mortgage. Not-for-Profit housing counseling agencies, including those approved by HUD, will offer free or low-cost housing counseling to you.

"It is important for you to be very careful when refinancing... because in some instances it can be more harmful than beneficial."

HUD approved housing counseling agencies will not give you monetary assistance, but they can and will be of tremendous help in setting up a dialogue between you and the Mortgage Company, which may lead to you keeping your house. You can contact the mortgage company yourself, or do so with the assistance of a housing counselor if you are not sure what to say or how to say the right thing. You can locate an approved housing counseling agency by contacting HUD (go to ***www.hud.gov*** or look under *U.S. Government* in the White Pages of your local phone book), asking your lender, or calling your local housing authority or office. It is a little known fact that Mortgage Service Companies and Mortgage Companies alike have workout departments which have been established to help in the event you have problems making your mortgage payments. Don't discount their ability to help you retain ownership of your house.

Refinancing: If you are considering refinancing as an option do not make a decision until you have met with a housing or credit counselor first to ensure someone not emotionally involved, and who is an expert in the field, advises you as to the potential benefit or harm such a transaction may bring. Refinancing when a property is at risk of foreclosure may seem like a good idea, and it may in fact be a useful alternative if your credit is reasonably good and you have equity in the property. It is important for you to be very careful when refinancing however, because in some instances it can be more harmful than beneficial.

There are mortgage companies which will make an effort to "take" your house from you if they so much as perceive the possibility exists. You may find you are digging a hole deeper than you can imagine. Be very careful when looking for a way to relieve yourself of oppressive debt. Refinancing may be a good choice, and it may not be. Take the time to discuss the matter with several mortgage companies, a housing counselor, or credit counselor. Your objective is to reduce your debt and save your house, so don't forget that while you are making decisions.

Depending on your circumstances, refinancing may be a good option if you do it with your eyes wide open and understand all the ramifications of the transaction. Remember, one of the net effects of a refinance is you are re-starting the loan from the beginning This is a good idea if it helps save the house. It is *not* a good idea if it only succeeds in getting you deeper into debt and worsens your situation.

Analyzing Refinancing Options: Before the refinancing process is begun, you should consider the following factors:

- **Unsecured and Secured Debts:** Unsecured debts are those which do not have collateral securing the loan. Examples of unsecured debts are medical bills, credit cards, lawyer fees, utilities, and hospital bills. These debtors must to go to court in order to recover their money. In most instances, the amount of the debt is not worth going to court to seek recovery. Secured loans are those in which someone has a collateral interest. The collateral might be house, a car, or other types of personal property pledged as security.

- **Interest Rates:** When you experience financial problems you become a high-risk debtor. If you refinance your loan, the new lender will charge you a higher interest rate, additional points, and may include penalties for early payment (a pre-payment penalty), along with insurance charges and other mechanisms designed to ensure the loan's repayment. For this reason, refinancing or loan consolidation often converts low-cost debts into high-cost debts. If you wish to refinance your house be aware most bank or mortgage company loans have lower finance rates/charges when compared to finance company loans. In general a bank loan should not be refinanced with a finance company loan, i.e. companies which may allow you to make retail purchases with no payments and no interest for ninety days or, seen from another angle, one of those storefront lenders sometimes referred to as "Consumer Lending Companies."

- **Adjustable Rate Mortgage:** A mortgage where the interest rate will be adjusted at specific predetermined periods of time; annually, every three, five or ten years, and sometimes even monthly. ARMS are not to be taken lightly. If you are considering one you really should seek the advice of a HUD certified counselor to confirm it is the best option for you. Most ARM base rates change based on pre-selected interest rate indexes which are disclosed in your loan documents - and should be very well understood by you.

- **Negative Amortization Loan**: This is one of the mortgage products most likely to cause financial problems for homeowners, especially if they are not fully aware of all of its features. *Neg Am* loans are Adjustable Rate Mortgages where your balance could possibly *escalate* instead of going down. These are very complicated loans, and in some cases there may be two interest rates. One is the actual rate, and one is the payment rate. The payment rate is usually considerably lower than the actual rate, and there is the potential for the difference between the two to be added to the balance of your mortgage.

- **Balloon Loan Payments:** A balloon loan is one where the mortgage payment is amortized over a longer specific period of time, but full payment of the entire balance is due within a specific shorter term. For example, a mortgage can be calculated with a thirty year repayment term, although the full balance would be due and payable in five years with the 60th monthly interest payment.

- **Up-Front Charges:** When a loan is refinanced you may have to pay points, broker's fees, and other up-front charges.

> **"Do not ever put your house at risk in order to save some other item of far less value."**

Remember, you already paid these charges as part of the original loan, so paying them all over again may make the refinanced loan more expensive depending on the amount of the loan and any additional fees or charges.

- **Pre-Payment Penalties:** Some mortgage loans have what are called *pre-payment penalties* which are due if you choose to end the loan before a pre-determined period of time has elapsed. The amount of the penalty will be determined by the mortgage and note agreement with the Mortgage Company. The term for a pre-payment penalty can vary from a few months to a few years. In other words you could owe as many as six monthly payments, typically expressed as interest payments, to cover the penalty. A prepayment penalty is triggered when the loan is repaid, or paid down, earlier than the mortgage documents allow. This can also happen if you re-finance or sell.

Deciding When Refinancing is an Option for You: Refinancing a home will always include charges and additional costs, and these extra costs may make your existing financial situation worse. Even so, when you are in financial crisis, you may have debt collectors urging you to refinance because in many cases they can only recover their money through some form of collateral such as your home. You should not let them pressure you into refinancing, because you may be putting your most important asset at risk. It is very difficult for a debt collector to repossess a household good, but it is easy for a refinancing institution to seize the collateral (i.e. the home) if payment is not received. This of course pre-supposes there has been a lien placed on the property as a result of the re-finance. Do not ever put your house at risk in order to save some other item of far less value. If given the choice of a re-finance or the loss of an item, losing the item may be the best alternative - even though it may be painful. It is usually better to lose an item than risk potentially losing your home. It is a matter of priorities.

In a perfect world the most valid reason for refinancing a long-term first mortgage is to get a significantly lower interest rate and a length of time roughly equivalent to that of the original loan. If you find such a package you should still evaluate the loan's hidden costs, fees, and any other costly clauses and terms. Take the time to review the loan before signing it. Remember, you have the right to decide to stop the refinancing process at any time before the closing, and even after the closing federal law gives the consumer three days to cancel for any reason. This is called a *rescission period,* and no money will be disbursed until three days have elapsed. Make sure to factor this into your plan.

Avoiding Predatory Lending Practices: If you are in a distressed condition or being threatened with foreclosure, you are likely to be exposed to unscrupulous firms which may want to take advantage of your financial crisis. You have to be on the alert to avoid false or misleading programs which are advertised as "the" remedy for foreclosure. You should be skeptical of *any* firm which contacts you about refinancing or loan consolidation. Firms soliciting loans via "door-to-door" sales and even mass mailings are not always trustworthy. In the United States mailings have become very creative, and in some cases unscrupulous companies come very close to representing themselves as government officials or even your mortgage lender in order to get your attention.

"Avoid any offer to sell your home with an option to buy it back."

If you have doubts about a firm you should check the business's name with your state attorney general, the banking commission, or the local consumer complaint hotline. Never sign documents, especially those related to your home, without fully comprehending what is contained in them. You should also avoid any offer to sell your home with an option to buy it back. Selling your home means giving up your rights as a homeowner. Be careful of advertised schemes to save your home from foreclosure, or personal solicitations to help you avoid it. Never, ever send an application or processing fee to a lender or servicer who advertises "Bad Credit, No Problem" and then provides a toll free (800, 888, or 877) or toll (900) number for you to call.

You may see signs along the road which advertise "I/WE WILL BUY YOUR HOME ANY CONDITION!" These companies or individuals *will* buy your house, but they will make an offer for a value far below what the normal market will support - in other words, an amount far less than the actual amount your house is worth.

Any proposal from a company seeking to consolidate all of your debts into one loan should be carefully analyzed before being accepted. Loans involving contractor fraud usually include a balloon payment, multiple refinancing, a high interest rate, high loan broker fees, credit insurance, excessive points, excessively high late charges, prepayment penalties, or high closing costs.

Mortgage Insurance Companies: As an additional step, or even as a last resort, you may want to consider contacting your Mortgage Insurance Company if you have mortgage insurance (some non-conforming mortgages don't have it), as they have a stake in your success or failure as well. Neither the MI Company nor the Mortgage Company wants to take your home. They aren't real estate companies, and have no wish to manage or dispose of your foreclosed property. Don't misunderstand this statement - they *will* if there is no other choice, because they must protect their legal position. The MI Company has a financial interest in helping you remain in the house and in keeping the mortgage alive and viable. In the event you fail to make your mortgage payments and the loan goes into default, the Mortgage Company will file a claim against the Mortgage Insurance Company for partial repayment of their loss.

The MI Company will encourage both the borrower and the lender to "work out" their difficulties if at all possible. The MI Company will advocate reinstatement of the loan if you have the ability to bring the mortgage current. Although the Mortgage Company may not open a dialogue on an *assumption*, when the situation permits the MI and mortgage companies may work together to allow an assumption by a properly qualified third party. This would have to be an "Arms Length" assumption, which means it can't be a relative or anyone who may have a financial interest in the family. The transaction would involve totally disinterested parties. Typically the documentation required would be a new mortgage application and proof of income in the form of Verifications of Employment or paystubs, and the MI Company must give its approval to any assumption presented for consideration.

Another option which may be offered by the MI company is a *Modification,* wherein the MI company allows the lender to in effect re-arrange the loan in certain ways to better enable you to afford your mortgage payment. This might involve reducing the interest rate, and if there are late charges or fees the MI Company may allow them to be included in the changes made to the loan.

OPTIONS IF YOU ARE IN DEFAULT

"If I were asked to give what I consider the single most useful bit of advice for all humanity it would be this: Expect trouble as an inevitable part of life and when it comes, hold your head high, look it squarely in the eye and say, "I will be bigger than you! You cannot defeat me!" - Ann Landers

OPTIONS IF YOU ARE IN DEFAULT

Several options may be available if you're in default on your mortgage. Many of the industry terms may be used interchangeably, although the specific option or "tool" available may vary by the type of mortgage, i.e. FHA, VA, conventional, etc. Almost all types of mortgages contain provisions for the following general options: forbearance agreements, reinstatement plans, and loan modifications. These options may assist you in curing the delinquency, retaining home ownership, and preventing foreclosure. The final decision regarding any help available to you will be made by the "Investor" or note holder. Their decision will be based in part on your previous payment history, current debt load, and other factors which will indicate your likely ability to repay the loan if they provide a way out.

All mortgage types contain several alternatives which may be available to you. Although you may not be able to retain ownership, you can attempt to mitigate the consequences of a foreclosure by utilizing one of the following options: pre-foreclosure sale, short sale or compromise offer, loan assumption, or a deed-in-lieu of foreclosure.

The following contains information on some of the options available to you if you are in default.

First and foremost, you should contact the Lender/Servicer and make a good faith effort to resolve the problem. Before initiating contact, go over your current bills and tally up your income. Prioritize what needs to be paid, and when. Eliminate any excess, and reduce your expenses so that you are in a position to show the Lender/Servicer you have taken stock of your situation and are making a good faith effort to reduce spending. You must have some type of plan to make good on your promise to repay, and it may require that you make difficult decisions.

Negotiating a Workout Agreement: In most cases, lenders/servicers are willing to negotiate a workout agreement with you in order to prevent foreclosure. Such an agreement may include a variety of options. If you are in default you will need assistance in analyzing the different alternatives available, and should consult a housing counseling agency for information, options and referrals.

Aggressive intervention is, in most cases, essential to protecting your interests. The neighborhood legal services office, a bar association panel of pro bono attorneys, or a program which provides legal assistance for the indigent are all possible sources of legal help. You should avoid "quick fix" attorneys who may advertise or solicit on television or through the mail. If you choose to postpone seeking professional assistance you could lose some of your important legal rights and may increase the costs of reinstating the loan.

Debt Repayment Plans: One option if you are in default is to establish a repayment plan agreement. Two main issues are considered in developing a repayment plan: future payments, and past due payments (also called arrears). In one type of repayment plan you agree to make monthly mortgage payments as they are due, together with a partial monthly payment on the arrears balance. For example, you may be able to pay one and one-fourth of the monthly payments for a predetermined length of time until the loan is current. This type of plan is recommended when you have a temporary financial crisis and can afford to pay some extra money in your monthly payment. Of course if you are having or have had financial problems for several months, you may not be in a position to make such payments. Instead, you may ask the lender or servicer for a temporary interest rate or payment reduction. You can ask the Lender/Servicer to do a variety of things, but anything you agree to do must be in writing. Further, you may be asked to show proof that you have the ability to make good on any agreement you enter into.

Mortgage Modification: A mortgage modification, also referred to as *recasting*, is the legal act of changing any of the terms of a mortgage so that you may avoid foreclosure after defaulting. For example, you and the lender might agree to a lower interest rate if the existing rate is higher than what they currently charge new customers, i.e. you have a 9% or 10% rate and the current market rates are 6% to 7%. The investor may agree to this as a means of maintaining a good loan and not seeing it go into default. This is not an option which is widely available, and some servicers typically never offer it to their customers - but in a difficult situation they may agree.

Other modification agreements might extend the length of the mortgage while lowering monthly payments, or convert an adjustable-rate mortgage to a fixed-rate mortgage or vice versa. The intent of a modification is to eliminate the loan's arrearage (past due payments) and reduce the monthly mortgage obligation when you have recovered from your financial distress - but your net income has been reduced to a level lower than it was prior to the default.

Partial Claim: This option, which is primarily used with FHA loans, is intended to help cure a default if the loan is at least 4 months but no more than 12 months in arrears. The loan must not be in foreclosure at the time that the Partial Claim is executed. In order to qualify for a Partial Claim the homeowner must demonstrate that he has overcome the cause that led to default, have sufficient income to resume monthly mortgage payments and be committed to continue to occupy the property as their primary residence.

A Partial Claim is a non-interest bearing promissory note that is issued to reinstate the loan. This note becomes due and payable when the mortgagor either pays off the first mortgage or no longer owns the property. A partial Claim may be utilized as a stand-alone tool or in conjunction with a special forbearance plan. A Partial Claim cannot be used in conjunction with a Loan Modification. Although Partial Claim has been primarily used for FHA loans, more and more conventional lenders are considering using Partial Claim.

Special Forbearance: A forbearance agreement allows you to make lower payments, or no payment at all, for a certain number of months (usually two to six). To make up for the missed payments, the next two to six installments will be higher, or the mortgage may be extended. Special forbearance requires the lender or servicer to refrain from continued foreclosure action beyond the timeframe in which foreclosure would ordinarily be initiated, i.e. the lender agrees to cease their action to foreclose until you either complete the terms of the forbearance or fail to do so. You may be considered for special forbearance provided:

- You have recently experienced an involuntary reduction in income or an increase in living expenses, and

- The lender determines you have a reasonable ability to eliminate the arrearage under the terms of the forbearance plan.

Capitalization: This is the process of applying delinquent amounts to the outstanding principal balance of a mortgage. This could be done by agreement of the lender if they are making an attempt to help you restructure the loan. They could allow the unpaid interest and fees to be added back into the loan, generally if you are less than six to twelve months past due.

Pre-Foreclosure Sale: Although becoming a more and more acceptable practice in the conventional loan arena, a pre-foreclosure sale is a term normally used when referring to an FHA mortgage and is an option which allows you to sell your property for less than the amount owed in order to avoid foreclosure. It may also be used when you owe less than the value of the home, but due to market forces or other conditions affecting the marketplace where the property is located you are not able to sell the house using normal methods. This process is sometimes referred to as a *short sale,* although that is most commonly used in reference to mortgages offered through the conventional industry. In cases involving a VA mortgage, these are referred to as *compromise offers*. The offer to Sell Short may be used with FHA mortgages or conventional mortgages. In the case of FHA mortgages, the Federal Housing Administration reimburses the lender's or servicer's expenses for the sale of a property to a third party in lieu of foreclosure. The VA or Veterans Administration may reimburse the lender where VA loans are at risk. In both situations the seller must visit a HUD housing counselor and discuss the sale of the house before entering into a final contract to sell, and a certificate must be issued to the seller and to FHA/VA as proof the counseling has taken place. The seller states they understand the action they are taking will lead to the loss of their house, and that there will be no compensation to them as a result.

For conventional mortgages, an agreement to execute a pre-foreclosure sale needs to be reached by the investor, the mortgage insurer, and the "owner." Lenders or servicers have the option of resolving incurable defaults by offering you this choice. If you cannot meet your mortgage obligation, the opportunity to sell your property through this alternative may be available. If you agree to sell your property(s) using this method you are relieved of your mortgage obligation, and may receive assistance toward seller-paid closing costs.

If you are selling short you also agree to give up any equity which may exist. There is the reality that, if you are selling short, there is nothing you can do to cure the arrears - so the lender has agreed to accept less as a final payment to reduce their potential losses. Hence the term "short sale."

Short Sale: The hot new "buzzword" on the lips of Realtors® today is *Short Sale,* and with all the hype surrounding the term one would think it is the biggest thing to hit the market since sliced bread. Short sales have been around for many years, and are a viable option for some people under some circumstances - but may not be the cure all for your mortgage ills. When you are considering the possibility of doing a short sale, the first thing to understand is you will not be in control of the process of accepting or rejecting offers. Your Realtor® needs to understand the process as well, because selling a house under short sale conditions is not quite the same as a standard real estate transaction.

Although it is not required for you to meet with a HUD housing counselor it is highly recommended, and you should invite whichever Realtor® you intend to use along as well. Your Realtor® can be an invaluable ally in this process, or turn out to be your worst nightmare if they don't know what their responsibilities are to both you and the mortgage company.

Have the Realtor® come out and conduct a *Brokers Price Opinion* (BPO) or *Comparable Market Analysis* (CMA) to obtain a relative value for the home. Your mortgage company may also perform a standard appraisal, and will certainly perform a home inspection to ensure "their" investment is being taken care of. The expenses for both will be added to the final cost to close on the house when sold.

The first step in the short sale process is to discuss the matter with your mortgage company. They must be notified of your intent to sell the house "short," or in the case of FHA or VA conduct a pre-foreclosure sale. Do not expect the mortgage company to simply say "Ok, go ahead and do what you want." They will most likely tell you to go forward with a formal listing of the property with a Realtor®, and to make every effort to sell the house for as close to market value as possible. After the property has been on the market for a minimum of of sixty to ninety days, and if no offers have come in during that period, the mortgage company may then be willing to accept less should an offer come to them.

The mortgage company will not tell you to stop making your payments, and neither will we. The lender wants you to make every effort to remain in the home, and will not encourage you to leave in most cases. Under the conditions of a short sale they typically want you to remain in the home until the house is sold, and will at that time give you instructions to leave after or just prior to closing. Only after the house is listed and has been on the market for a period of time with no offers coming in will the mortgage company allow you to instruct the Realtor® to reduce the listing price. Always keep in mind that if the final sales price accepted by the mortgage company is less than what you owe, you may be responsible for the difference. A HUD certified housing counselor can explain the consequences relevant to your particular situation.

"Always keep in mind that if the final sales price accepted by the mortgage company is less than what you owe, you may be responsible for the difference."

When the house is sold, or as offers are brought, they are sent directly to the mortgage company by the listing agent. All offers should be free of typical contingencies such as the seller (owner) paying closing costs, thereby allowing for creative financing such as seller-held second mortgages. The seller is typically not allowed to accept any conditions on the sale, as all offers will be accepted or rejected by the mortgage company.

It will take from forty-five to sixty days for the mortgage company to give an approval on a "short sale," so the homeowner and new buyer should have patience with the process. If the seller has an FHA mortgage, they must be seen by a HUD certified housing counselor and the proper forms completed and sent to the mortgage company before the contract is allowed to close. The purpose of this counseling and signed documentation is to ensure the seller is fully aware of their role in the process, and that in most cases their house is being sold with them taking no funds from the transaction.

You will not walk away with any funds from the closing. The whole meaning of a short sale is the lender loses money in the transaction. Selling short provides you with a way out, but it requires the lender to take less than they would normally accept to retire the loan. One of the reasons they are willing to do this is it prevents foreclosure, which could cost them even *more* money than the short sale. Keep in mind the lender does not have to accept any short offer if they deem it too low. The lender is the final decision making authority in all matters related to your mortgage, and you must take this into account as you weigh your options.

Once an offer is accepted the seller is notified that the property is to be sold and given a general time to vacate. This could be as much as thirty days, because it is in the mortgage company's best interest to keep the house occupied until it has a new owner and occupant. The mortgage company

"There are scams taking place around Short Sales, so be careful you aren't engaging in a "Flip for Profit" scheme which encourages the sale in an attempt to defraud the lender."

does not have unlimited patience, and will not wait forever before taking action. If the house does not sell they may decide they have no other choice but to continue on to foreclosure. It is for this reason you should participate as actively as possible in the sale. Keep the house as presentable as possible, and make it available for showing as often as possible –

even on short notice. Don't make your Realtor's®
job difficult and the house difficult to sell.

From your perspective, one of the most important reasons to approach the lender with a sort sale in mind is the impact on you the home owner may be less damaging from a credit perspective. That is to say, you may be able to position yourself to purchase another home more quickly after a short sale as compared to a foreclosure. Lenders are now treating Short Sales much differently than most other remedies available, and may allow a homeowner who has lost their home in a Short Sale to re-purchase again in approximately two to three years as compared to the typical five or more. Steps to put you back on track to purchase again are outlined in the *Rebuilding Your Credit* chapter of this book.

There are scams taking place around Short Sales, so be careful you aren't engaging in a "Flip for Profit" scheme which encourages the sale in an attempt to defraud the lender. Do not follow the advice of a "company or individual" who is telling you to ask the lender to agree to a short sale so you and they can sell the property at a lower price, they can re-purchase the house at that lower price, and then sell it back to you. This is illegal!

"You will not walk away with any funds from the closing."

What to Send Your Lender When Asking For a Short Sale:

- **Letter of Authorization:** A notarized letter including your name, property address, loan reference number, date and Realtor® name and contact information.
- **Financial Statement:** Lenders want to know if you have savings accounts, money market accounts, stocks and bonds, negotiable instruments, cash, or other real estate or anything of value.
- **Net Sheet** – The lender will want the realtor to prepare an itemized breakdown of costs associated with the sale before approving a short sale
- **Proof of Income and Assets:** Copies of your last two years tax returns with W-2's and all tax schedules, together with your two most recent monthly pay stubs.
- **Bank Statements:** If your bank statements reflect unaccountable deposits, large cash

withdrawals or an unusual number of checks, it's probably a good idea to explain each of those line items to your lender

- **CMA:** A Comparable Market Analysis (CMA) prepared by your Realtor® should accompany your documentation. It should include active, pending, and the last six months history of homes sold in your area.

- **Purchase Contract:** Send this along with an earnest money receipt and the loan approval letter for a new buyer after you receive an offer.

- **Hardship Letter:** Briefly describes the reason(s) you are unable to make your mortgage payments and indicates whether you expect the problem to be short or long term.

Compromise Offer: This term is often used when discussing a VA pre-foreclosure sale. This compromise agreement allows the VA (Veterans Administration) to pay the lender the difference between the sale proceeds and the mortgage balance (but not in excess of the original guarantee) and is often appropriate when the property value is less than the existing loan balance. The VA guarantees the mortgage lender will be made whole in the event of a veteran's default. This option is generally only available from the VA, and must have been negotiated in advance of any action. There is no guarantee the VA will allow this as a way out for the borrower, so don't make commitments on their behalf. The borrower should also be prepared to meet with a HUD housing counselor to discuss the PFS or Pre-Foreclosure Short Sale.

"Assumptions of mortgage loans are rare, and should not be seen as either an easy or quick way out."

Assumption: Assumption is a term used for the method of transferring property to a new buyer who agrees to take responsibility for (assume) an existing mortgage. While some mortgages are assumable, most are not because they include a due-on-sale provision. This provision allows a lender or servicer to call a loan due and payable (for the remaining balance) if ownership of the mortgaged property is transferred, however if you are in default you may be granted a waiver by the lender or servicer on a case-by-case basis if sale or transfer of the property will prevent a foreclosure. Assumptions of mortgage loans are rare, and should not be seen as either an easy or quick way out. In most cases an assumption will not be allowed, so it is in your best interest to keep your other options open at all times.

Deed-In-Lieu of Foreclosure: If you have defaulted on your mortgage loan you may be given an opportunity to voluntarily return the property to the foreclosing lender or servicer, which will stop the foreclosure. This option requires the permission of the lender or servicer. If they accept this option, you (the borrower) and the lender will sign a deed-in-lieu of foreclosure. This document transfers the property from you (the borrower) to the lender or servicer. Remember, you are relinquishing your rights to any and all equity or other proceeds derived from the future sale of the property.

Choosing The Deed-In-Lieu Of Foreclosure: This alternative is recommended if you believe the property is not worth saving and your circumstances meet most of the following criteria:

- You have no equity, or there is negative equity in the property.

- The local Real Estate market is marginally strong, rather than weak or declining.

- You have no money to afford scheduled loan payments, even if the foreclosure is stopped.

- You do not want to have a foreclosure on your credit report.

Benefits of A Deed-In-Lieu of Foreclosure: Both you and the lender/servicer can benefit from of a deed-in-lieu of foreclosure. The first benefit is immediate cessation of the foreclosure process - the property will not be sold at a foreclosure sale. As a result your credit is partially protected, although it has certainly been adversely affected by the missing payments. Even so, a foreclosure sale would likely ruin what is left of your credit for many years to come.

In some states, when the deed-in-lieu of foreclosure is agreed upon, it is possible you will no longer be responsible for paying the balance of the loan regardless of the property's resale value - thus becoming immune to deficiency judgments.

The lender/servicer may have the benefit of acquiring immediate title to the property with no additional costs or delays. They may also avoid the uncertainty of waiting to see if you will file a lawsuit to enjoin the trustee's sale, file bankruptcy, or use some other strategy to stop the foreclosure. It is important to note that mortgagees are not immune from possible deficiency judgments in all states.

Negotiating A Deed-In-Lieu Of Foreclosure: Before agreeing to a deed-in lieu of foreclosure, you should negotiate the following points with the lender or servicer:

- Is the lender/servicer going to cancel the mortgage note or deed of trust?
- Will the lender/servicer allow you to continue to occupy the property for any period of time until you can find a new home? If the answer is yes be clear as to the actual amount of time, if any, which will be allowed, and if there will be any cost.
- Will the lender/servicer reflect the deed-in-lieu on your credit report promptly, and over what period of time? Keep in mind it may take from thirty to ninety days for this information to appear in your credit profile.
- Is the lender/servicer willing to waive a deficiency judgment? This is any amount left over after the sale and a balance still exists, and may only be known after the property has been sold to a new buyer.

IS BANKRUPTCY AN OPTION?

"Always bear in mind that your own resolution to succeed is more important than any other one thing."

- Abraham Lincoln

IS BANKRUPTCY AN OPTION?

Another option a homeowner facing foreclosure should consider is bankruptcy, although this path contains potential pitfalls if you do not know how to navigate the legal system. It will also have a negative impact on your credit. We strongly recommend you contact a legal professional to discuss the pros and cons of filing bankruptcy to see if it is the right option for your particular situation. Although a detailed discussion of the bankruptcy option is well beyond the scope of this book, the following is a short explanation of the process.

The bankruptcy process is governed by federal law, rather than state law. If you file bankruptcy, a foreclosure proceeding will be "stayed" pending the outcome of the bankruptcy or until your mortgage company obtains a "relief from stay" to allow it to proceed against your property. This means once you file a bankruptcy in *federal* court your mortgage company cannot proceed with its foreclosure action in *state* court until the bankruptcy is completed, discharged, dismissed, or the mortgage company obtains permission from the federal court to continue with the action. At a minimum the bankruptcy option will buy a homeowner additional time and prolong the foreclosure process.

TYPES OF BANKRUPTCY

There are two bankruptcy options available to a distressed homeowner. The homeowner may file a Chapter 7 Bankruptcy, or a Chapter 13. It must be noted that in 2005 bankruptcy laws changed to require applicants to attend a government approved credit counseling program before being able to file either a Chapter 7 or Chapter 13. The next section discusses this new requirement in more depth. It also addresses relatively new rules governing how much time must pass before a distressed homeowner who has already filed bankruptcy once before must wait before being eligible to file again.

- **Chapter 7:** A Chapter 7 Bankruptcy, also known as "liquidation," involves your non-exempt property being sold for the benefit of your creditors and your unsecured debts (such as your credit cards) being discharged. In 2005 a new requirement was added that one must qualify under the Chapter 7 *Means Test* prior to filing a Chapter 7 Bankruptcy. This option will prolong the foreclosure process, but it will not ultimately prevent the foreclosure of your home. As noted above, when you file a Chapter 7 Bankruptcy in federal court, the foreclosure process will cease until your property is sold by the bankruptcy trustee or, more likely, when the mortgage company obtains permission from the federal court ("relief from the bankruptcy stay") to continue with its foreclosure action. A Chapter 7 bankruptcy will buy you some time, but it will not ultimately prevent the foreclosure of your home.

- **Chapter 13:** A Chapter 13 Bankruptcy involves the repayment of mortgage arrears and other debt through future income rather than from the liquidation sale of your assets. Under a Chapter 13 Bankruptcy plan, you are basically entering into a payment plan for the repayment of your debts. To qualify for this bankruptcy option, you will need to be employed or have a regular source of income, you must have sufficient income to meet your living expenses (which will include your monthly mortgage payments) as well as the plan payments, and you must not have debt in excess of the statutory caps for a Chapter 13Bankruptcy. The Chapter 13 Bankruptcy plan can last up to 3 to 5 years. As long as you are making payments under the plan and making your monthly mortgage payment, your mortgage company cannot contact you regarding your pre-bankruptcy filing mortgage arrears. This plan offers the homeowner much needed time to get back on track and, if enough time goes by, it may also permit a homeowner time to refinance on more favorable terms. However, if the homeowner fails to make current monthly mortgage payments or payments under the plan, then the mortgage company will attempt to obtain permission from the federal court ("relief from the bankruptcy stay") to continue with its foreclosure action. If you are considering the bankruptcy option, we strongly urge you to contact a qualified legal professional who can advise you whether this option is right for you under your particular circumstances, and which bankruptcy option is best suited for your situation. The bankruptcy option has consequences (such as negatively affecting your credit score) and it has complex rules such as filing requirements and time deadlines. Given this, it is in your best interest to consult with a qualified legal professional before pursuing this option.

"...consult with a qualified legal professional before pursuing (bankruptcy)."

> **“In a Chapter 7, the automatic stay will *temporarily* prevent the lender from foreclosing.”**

New Bankruptcy Law Requires Credit Counseling Before Filing: Since October 17, 2005, consumers filing for bankruptcy have been required to go through a government-approved credit counseling program within six months before filing for bankruptcy protection.

The Federal Trade Commission suggests important questions for consumers to ask when reviewing the state-by-state list of government-approved credit counseling organizations listed on the DOJ website (**www.usdoj.gov/ust**) – including inquiries about fees, counselor training, and services offered.

The required counseling can take place in person, over the phone, or online. Consumers can expect the session to last about ninety minutes and include an analysis of their budget. While the organization can charge a reasonable fee for its services (as much as fifty dollars depending on location, services offered, and administrative costs) organizations approved by the government must waive the fee for anyone who cannot afford to pay. After the counseling is complete consumers must get a certificate as proof;

which some organizations may charge extra for. Consumers should check to ensure they will receive the correct certificate for the bankruptcy court where they will be filing.

Credit counseling organizations advise consumers on managing money, and debts, and developing a budget. Most offer free educational materials and workshops, and sometimes they may recommend and negotiate a debt management plan (DMP) for their clients. In a DMP consumers deposit money each month with the credit counseling organization, which then uses the funds to pay off debts according to a schedule worked out with the consumers and their creditors. A DMP is not required for consumers who are filing for bankruptcy, but if one is used a copy of the plan must be provided to the bankruptcy court when filing.

For more information about other changes in the bankruptcy law and how they affect consumers visit ***www.usdoj.gov/ust/bapcpa/index.htm***. For more information about credit issues and choosing a credit counselor, ***visit www.ftc.gov/credit***.

Copies of the consumer alert are available from the FTC's Web site at ***http://www.ftc.gov*** and from the FTC's Consumer Response Center, Room 130, 600 Pennsylvania Avenue N.W., Washington, D.C. 20580. The FTC works for the consumer to prevent fraudulent, deceptive, and unfair business practices in the marketplace, and to provide information to help consumers spot, stop, and avoid them. To file a complaint in English or Spanish (bilingual counselors are available to take complaints), or to get free information on any of 150 consumer topics, call toll-free, 1-877-FTC-HELP (1-877-382-4357), or use the complaint form at ***http://www.ftc.gov***. The FTC enters internet, telemarketing, identity theft, and other fraud-related complaints into *Consumer Sentinel*, a secure online database available to hundreds of civil and criminal law enforcement agencies in the U.S. and abroad.

MANAGING A FINANCIAL CRISIS

"I say to myself, I've lived through this and can take the next thing that comes along . . . We must do the things we think we cannot do."

- Eleanor Roosevelt

If your household income has changed very real questions must be asked, and a difficult situation must be addressed. Answer the following questions: Are you in a position to keep your house? What, if anything, are you willing and/or able to do to keep it?

Do you have reserves in the bank? When a mortgage is in or about to go into default, it is usually because of a lack of cash or cash flow in the household. This is the time homeowners are most likely to be susceptible to scams and questionable offers of "help."

> **"...your *Crisis Budget* may be quite different from your normal one."**

Establish A Crisis Budget: Income and expense budgeting is important for everyone, but it is *especially* important if you are in a financial crisis. A budget is, of course, a list of anticipated income and expected expenses, but your *Crisis Budget* may be quite different from your normal one. A crisis budget will include contingencies for a sudden reduction in or loss of income, and may have a provision for a major debt which comes out of nowhere or provisions for the other unanticipated circumstances which are a part of life.

Making a budget plan will help you identify your current spending practices which may be a result of impulse, trustfulness, or low sales resistance. It will help guide you in spending money on what is really needed, and in prioritizing your debts according to your family's needs. A sample budget can be found in the Resource Guide of this book, or you may visit ***www.myhomeamerica.org*** for an interactive online tool which will guide you in setting up a budget.

If you have never before made a budget plan, it is best to begin by writing down present income and current expenses. A sample *Budget*, or *Income and Expense Worksheet*, can be found in the Forms section of this book. Ask yourself these questions:

- What are the present sources of my income?
- What will these sources be in the future?
- What are my current spending patterns?
- Is it possible to make changes in these spending practices in order to reduce expenses?
- Do I expect more expenses in the future?
- What can be done to improve my income?

- What strategies would I use to pay off debts if my income became more limited?

It is likely analyzing these questions will lead you to conclude some payments need to be postponed until the future. Your goal is to minimize the deficit between income and expenses. To do this, you will need to find ways to increase income and reduce expenses. Analyzing the financial decisions you made in the last couple of months before the financial crisis struck will provide you with material for comparison, and may help generate ideas about income expansion and expense reduction. You should continue to fill out and develop budget plans even after the crisis passes. If you are in a crisis now, it is recommended you seek the assistance of credit and housing counselors to prepare budget plans and prioritize the payment of your debts.

A crisis budget may look nothing like a normal budget. Where in the past you had funds earmarked for eating out and entertainment, these options are no longer part of the equation. Where you may have once had funds set aside for a vacation, that is no longer an option. You may have had money for new clothes, a new Plasma Screen TV, or an upgrade to a current entertainment system – for the time being these are out of the question.

Your priorities must change, along with everything else you once may have taken for granted regarding your spending. If you want to keep your house, your new priority must be to dedicate all of your funds toward paying and/or reinstating your mortgage. Your mortgage company will want to know they are your highest priority, and that no one will get paid before they do. This is vitally important if you intend to keep your house.

> **"Many people *say* they want to keep their house, but when it comes time to put the statement into action it's always "I'll do it later..."**

Many people *say* they want to keep their house, but when it comes time to put the statement into action it's always "I'll do it later." In other words they don't want to reduce their spending, save money, get another job, or work overtime. They weren't willing to do whatever was necessary to keep their home. Owning a house is a major obligation, and hopefully you are committed to doing whatever it takes - as long as "it is legal, ethical, and moral" - to keep it.

When your mortgage company/servicer requests a financial statement, it is important for you to be honest with them about what you earn and the obligations you pay. That financial statement will be used as a tool for determining your suitability for receiving help. That may sound harsh, but remember the purpose of the document is to establish your capacity to pay or re-pay an arrearage. A sample of such a form can be found in the Resource Section of this book.

The following are some items you may have to consider when planning a crisis budget, and the relevant consequences for delinquency with each.

Housing-Related Bills: Any payment associated with the home should be considered to be of the highest priority because not making them puts you at risk of losing your home. House-related bills include the mortgage payment (a full minimum payment including taxes and insurance if escrowed, or set aside 1/12th of the non-escrowed taxes and insurance each month if it is not), and fees for your taxes if they aren't included in the monthly payment along with insurance. Other expenses include maintenance fees for condominiums and townhouses if required and paid separately, along with Home Owners Association dues which may be paid on a separate statement and schedule. Not paying HOA dues can in many cases lead to legal action, and may result in foreclosure on its own.

Utility Services: Household utilities are considered essential to daily life, so they are a priority. When you are in financial distress you should ask about special discount programs which are available in most states. Talk to the utility company and discuss ways you may be able to reduce your utility bills. Establishing a "level payment program" may allow you to have a consistent monthly utility payment, making budgeting easier. Pay your bills on time and avoid late payment charges. Reduce your usage of utilities in general. Reset the thermostat to different settings so the air conditioner and/or heater run less often, change the filter regularly, keep windows covered with drapes or blinds, and turn off lights when rooms are not in use.

Car Loans: If your car is needed to get to work it should be treated as a priority, so pay the monthly car loan or lease. If you own more than one car, serious consideration should be given to eliminating one or more payments by selling any car which is not absolutely necessary. You may also consider selling an expensive car in order to buy a used or a less costly vehicle. Use of the car should be reduced to save money on gasoline and car maintenance. Car insurance payments should also be a high priority. These may seem like drastic suggestions, but remember the final objective is to keep your house. “Things” can be replaced once you are back on your feet.

Child Support Debts: Child support payments may be considered a primary need, since they are assigned for the purpose of providing food, health, and clothing. In some states, failing to pay child support is a criminal action punishable by a prison sentence. In other states missed child support payments may lead to suspension or revocation of driving privileges, making it more difficult to get to work.

Student Loans: You may be able to request a forbearance or suspension of payments in order to get back on your feet. Talk with your servicer about your situation, and let them know you are having difficulties. Ask if they will provide you some form of relief, but keep in mind there are no guarantees.
The government provides a number of options for you if you cannot afford to pay off a student loan, however it also has special powers to collect on such loans. They can seize up to ten percent of the wage of the debtor (that’s you) without a court order, and can charge up to forty-three percent in collection fees. For this reason, making student loan payments should be a medium priority.

Uncollateralized Loans: Some loans such as credit cards, health care debts, and open accounts with merchants are low priority for payment because they do not have any collateral behind them. If the creditor did require you to offer household goods such as furniture or an appliance as collateral and the loan defaults, they are usually not worth seizing because of their low market value and the court process for taking them may be too expensive for the creditor – although this may not be the case if you are on a rental plan. These types of loans may actually fall into the lowest priority, because in the grand scheme of things the house once again takes highest priority. When negotiating with the mortgage company for relief, you must be able to demonstrate your house is the largest priority in your financial life and will be paid for at the expense of all else. Understand this is *not* a blanket statement encouraging you to neglect paying your other bills. It is instead an honest statement based on experience gained from working with lenders and individuals in foreclosure.

MORTGAGE LOAN SERVICERS

"Let us never negotiate out of fear, but let us never fear to negotiate."

- John F. Kennedy

Communicating With The Mortgage Loan Servicer: A lack of understanding about the process of foreclosure, along with the distress and panic created by the threat of losing your home, may produce a tendency toward inaction. It is very important to understand that "acting on time" is essential to avoiding foreclosure. In most instances a delay in action may end up costing you your legal rights. You should call your mortgage institution as soon as you begin to have financial problems. By being the first to call, you establish your good faith in the eyes of the lender. There are many alternatives which can be discussed if you call early in the process. When communicating with the lender/servicer, keep the following in mind:

"You should call your mortgage institution as soon as you begin to have financial problems."

Identify Lender/Servicer: You first need to identify the lender or servicer to whom the monthly payment is owed. A servicing agent may be a bank, mortgage company, or other private corporation hired by the actual lender - sometimes referred to as the investor (after closing) - to service the loan. Servicing the loan includes collecting payments, issuing payment coupons and late notices, monitoring insurance and tax payments, dispersing payments as required, and handling foreclosure if necessary. Large national servicers often have different departments assigned to different stages of delinquency. Be aware that you will need to ask for the correct department so you do not waste time and effort talking to the wrong people. Some servicers have collection departments which serve multiple purposes, and others have separate departments established to serve specific functions. Conversely, you may find your servicer has a department which handles collections and loss mitigation all in one area. Your job is to determine who you are able to speak with, what their function may be, and most importantly how can they be of help in your current situation. Listen to what they say carefully, and don't overreact to anything you hear. We'll discuss more of the responses and actions you may want to take later.

Call The Lender/Servicer: You should keep a record of all telephone numbers with extensions and the names of the department(s), dates of calls, addresses, and names of your contacts. All written correspondence should be sent with return receipt requested as proof of delivery. When you begin to experience financial difficulty, you must call the appropriate division and explain the situation in detail. You should keep a record of this conversation, including the date and time of the call, the name of the person you talked to, and their response. If there are any initial agreements made during this call, write them down and keep ongoing records. Remember one important point. If you are talking to the collections department there is essentially only one response they can give you, and that is "Pay me what you owe me!" They have very few options available. The point here is at this stage you need not be discouraged. Listen to what they have to say, keeping in mind the collections department can only offer you the option of paying the arrearage and nothing more. It will be the *loss mitigation* department which can offer you the most options.

Write A Letter Of Explanation: Soon after making the initial phone call, write a letter explaining the reasons for the delay in payment. Make sure to reference the telephone call. Declare your willingness to continue to making payments on the home, based on your ability and their willingness to work with you. Restate any commitments or payment arrangements made with the collections department. Most importantly, state in clear unambiguous terms your desire to keep your house.

> **"...establish a paper trail which will help demonstrate that you are cooperating."**

Respond to Inquiries: It is vital for you respond to follow-up inquiries from the lender or servicer immediately. Do not avoid contact with them, no matter how difficult or unpleasant that contact may be. Instead, when you are having problems making your payments, you should aim to establish a paper trail which will help demonstrate that you are cooperating. Your lender/servicer will send you various types of correspondence. Read and respond to whatever you receive in the mail. Just a simple acknowledgement may be enough to keep the lines of communication open along with your options. Always let the servicer know you want to keep the house and will go the extra mile to work out your difficulties.

Your lender will typically send you information in the form of a letter giving directions on what to do and who to call to benefit from specific help.

This is standard procedure. Some lenders and servicers are now making a special effort to mitigate the anxiety surrounding delinquency and default by reaching out to low and moderate-income borrowers through Community Services Organizations, Community Based Not-for-Profits, and HUD approved housing counseling agencies. These agencies are in your neighborhood, and it may be a good idea to contact them and see what, if any, remedies are available to you either in the form of counseling or, in some very rare cases, even financial. The availability of such funds may be very limited, so please don't go in thinking that there is a safety net waiting for you. In most cases this will not be the case.

YOU MAY AVOID FORECLOSURE AND KEEP YOUR HOME

"We are continually faced by great opportunities brilliantly disguised as insolvable problems."

- Unknown

YOU MAY AVOID FORECLOSURE AND KEEP YOUR HOME

Losing a home can be financially and personally devastating. Here's information to help you keep your home. Relief may be available.

People facing financial problems: If you are facing unemployment or have money problems you may be able to keep your home if you know the right steps to take. Read on for important information and links to local organizations which can help you get through difficult times without losing your home.

Disaster area victims: If you live or work in an area declared a disaster by the President, and the hurricane, tornado, flood, wildfire, or other natural or man-made event damaged your home or reduced your income, your lender will provide disaster relief. In some cases you may not have to make a payment for ninety days or more.

Military personnel and their spouses: If you or your spouse is on active military duty you may qualify for a reduction in your interest rate resulting in lower payments. The Servicemembers' Civil Relief Act of 2003 (formerly the Soldiers' and

Sailors' Civil Relief Act of 1940) affects military homeowners.

Facing Financial Problems: Financial problems are most often associated with major life changes such as:

- Job loss
- Cuts in work hours or overtime
- Retirement
- Illness, injury, or death of a family member
- Divorce or separation

If your family is facing any of these issues and you can't pay your bills, look closely at what you owe and what you earn. Eliminate unnecessary spending and reach out for help if you still can't make ends meet. Taking action right away can help you protect your family from the loss of your home.

STEPS TO TAKE WHEN YOU CAN'T PAY YOUR MORTGAGE

Contact your lender as soon as you have a problem. Many people avoid calling lenders about money troubles because they:

- Feel embarrassed discussing money problems with others.

- Believe if lenders know they are in trouble, they will automatically rush to a collection agency or initiate foreclosure (seize property for failure to pay a mortgage debt)

Lenders want to *help* borrowers *keep* their homes because:

- Foreclosure is expensive for lenders, mortgage insurers, and investors

- HUD and private mortgage insurance companies and investors like Freddie Mac and Fannie Mae require lenders to work aggressively to help borrowers facing money problems.

Lenders have workout options (choices) to help you:

- These options work best when your loan is only one or two payments behind.

- Typically the *farther behind* you are on your payments, the *fewer options* are available.

Don't assume that your problems will quickly correct themselves:

- Don't lose valuable time being overly optimistic.

- Contact your mortgage lender to discuss your circumstances as soon as you realize you are unable to make your payments.

- Look forward to your lender being willing to explore many possible solutions, without guaranteeing any one in particular.

Finding Your Lender: Check the following sources to contact your lender:

- Your monthly mortgage billing statement.

- Your payment coupon book.

Information to Have Ready When You Call: To help you, lenders usually need:

- Your loan account number.
- Address of the property.
- SSN of borrower.
- A brief explanation of your circumstances.
- Recent income documents:

    - ✓ Pay stubs

    - ✓ Benefit statements from Social Security, disability, unemployment, retirement, or public assistance.

- ✓ Tax returns, or a year-to-date profit and loss statement if self-employed.
- ✓ A list of household expenses or financial statement.

Expect to have more than one phone conversation with your lender. Typically, your lender will mail you a "loan workout" package. This package contains information, forms, and instructions. If you want to be considered for assistance you must complete the forms fully and truthfully and return them to your lender quickly. Your lender will review the complete package before talking with you about a solution.

CALL YOUR LENDER TODAY! The sooner you call, the sooner help will be made available.

> **"If your lender doesn't hear from you, they will have no choice but to start legal action…"**

Don't Ignore Mail From Your Lender: If you don't get in touch with your lender, your lender will try to contact *you* by both mail and telephone soon after you stop making payments. It is very important that you respond. If your lender doesn't hear from you, they will have no choice but to start legal action leading to foreclosure, which will greatly increase the cost of bringing your loan current.

Information for Those with FHA Loans: The FHA provides many alternatives for borrowers who need help. These include mortgage modifications (changes), special forbearances (allowances), and other avenues to avoiding foreclosure.

FHA works closely with customers who have FHA-insured loans. If you feel your lender is not responding to your questions or need help contacting your lender, call them at (800) CALL-FHA.

Talk to a Housing Counselor: If you don't feel comfortable talking with your lender, you should immediately contact a housing counseling agency and make an appointment. Most HUD counselors are free, or cost very little. A counselor can help you:

- Review your financial situation, determine what options are available to you, and negotiate with your lender.

- Learn which of the various workout arrangements your lender may consider makes the most sense for you and your family based on your circumstances.

- Call the lender with you, or on your behalf, to discuss a workout plan.
- Protect you from future credit problems before you get too far behind on mortgage payments.
- Give you information on services and programs in your area which provide financial, legal, medical or other assistance.

A good counselor will help you create a monthly budget plan to ensure you meet all your monthly expenses, including your mortgage payment. Your personal financial plan will clearly show how much money you have available to make the mortgage payment. This analysis will help you and your lender determine whether a reduced or delayed payment schedule could help you.

To find out more about HUD-approved housing counseling agencies and their services visit ***www.hud.gov/offices/hsg/sfh/hcc/hcs.cfm*** or call toll free **(800) 569-4287** on weekdays between 9:00 AM and 5:00 PM Eastern Standard Time (6:00 AM to 2:00 PM PST). The same number can give you an automated referral to the three housing counseling agencies located closest to you.

Many of these local housing counseling agencies are connected with national and regional housing counseling intermediaries (mediators). The following website for HUD-approved national and regional housing counseling intermediaries describes the full range of assistance offered and provides maps showing their member's locations: ***www.hud.gov/offices/hsg/sfh/hcc/nrhci.cfm***

Prioritize Your Debts: Rank them by importance. As previously mentioned, you will need a new, streamlined budget if you lose your job or have an income change. Prioritize your bills, and pay those most necessary for your family: i.e. food, utilities and shelter.

Failing to pay any of your debts can seriously affect your credit rating, but if you stop making your *mortgage* payments you could lose your *house*. Try these suggestions in order to keep your home:

- Whenever possible use any income available, after paying for food and utilities, to pay your monthly mortgage payments.

- If your employment income has stopped or been reduced, first consider getting rid of or cutting back on other expenses such as dining out, entertainment, cable, or even telephone services.

- If you still do not have enough income, consider cashing out other financial resources such as stocks, savings accounts, or personal property which may have value like a boat or second car.

- Take any responsible action which will save cash.

Besides speaking with your lender, you may want to contact a nonprofit consumer credit counseling agency which specializes in helping restructure credit payments. Credit counselors can often reduce your monthly bills by negotiating lower payments or long-term payment plans with your creditors. Trustworthy credit counseling agencies provide their services free of charge, or for a small monthly fee tied to a repayment plan. Beware of credit counseling agencies which offer their services for a large upfront fee or donation. For consumer debt advice, visit ***www.debtadvice.org/*** on the web.

When you call a credit counseling agency, they will ask you to provide current information about your income and expenses. Be sure to find out if the agency has a charge *before* you sign any documents!

Preserve Your Good Credit: Do not underestimate or misjudge how important it is to maintain good credit. Your ability to purchase items, rent or buy a home, and do many other things often requires a credit check. Consumer credit agencies and your lender can help you explore ways to keep your credit from getting blemished.

Maintaining good credit is even important for job hunters. When you apply for a job, the employer will probably check your credit report to determine whether:

- You have been sued.
- You have filed for bankruptcy.
- You are having trouble paying your bills.

Explore Loan Workout Solutions With Your Lender: First and foremost, if you can keep your mortgage current, do so - but if in spite of your best efforts you find you are unable to make your mortgage payments, you might qualify for a loan workout option. Check with your lender to see which options may be available, because some may not apply to your loan if it is not insured by FHA.

If your problem is temporary call your lender to discuss these possibilities:

- **Reinstatement:** Your lender is always willing to discuss accepting the total amount owed in a lump sum by a specific date. Forbearance may accompany this option.

- **Forbearance:** Your lender may allow you to reduce or suspend payments for a short period of time and then agree to another option to bring your loan current. A forbearance option is often combined with a reinstatement when you know you will have enough money to bring the account current at a specific time. The money might come from a hiring bonus, investment, insurance settlement, or tax refund.

- **Repayment plan:** You may be able to get an agreement to resume making your regular monthly payments, plus a portion of the past due payments each month until you are caught up.

> **"... your lender may be willing to change the terms of your original loan to make the payments more affordable."**

If it appears that your situation is long-term or will permanently affect your ability to bring your account current, call your lender to discuss the following options:

- **Mortgage Modification:** If you can make payments on your loan, but don't have enough money to bring your account current or can't afford your current payment, your lender may be willing to change the terms of your original loan to make the payments more affordable. Your loan could be permanently changed in one or more of the following ways:

  ✓ Adding the missed payments to the existing loan balance.

  ✓ Changing the interest rate, including making an adjustable rate into a fixed rate.

  ✓ Extending the number of years you have to repay.

- **Partial Claim:** If your mortgage is insured your lender might help you get a one-time interest-free loan from your mortgage guarantor to bring your account current, and you may be allowed to wait several years before repaying it. You qualify for an FHA partial claim if:

  ✓ Your loan is between four and twelve months delinquent.

- ✓ You are able to begin making full mortgage payments again.

When your lender files a partial claim, HUD will pay them the amount necessary to bring your mortgage current. You must sign a promissory note, and a lien will be placed on your property until it is paid in full. The note is interest-free, and is due when you pay off the first mortgage or when you sell the property.

If keeping your home is not an option, call your lender to discuss these possibilities:

- **Sale:** If you can no longer afford your home, your lender will usually give you a specific amount of time to find a purchaser and pay off the total amount owed. You will be expected to use the services of a real estate professional who can aggressively market the property.
- **Pre-Foreclosure Sale or Short Payoff:** If you can't sell the property for the full amount of the loan, your lender may accept less than the amount owed. Financial help may also be available to pay other lien holders and/or help towards some moving costs. You may qualify if:

- ✓ The loan is at least two months delinquent.
- ✓ You or your real estate professional can sell the house within three to five months.
- ✓ A new appraisal obtained by your lender shows the value of your home meets HUD program guidelines.

- **Assumption:** A qualified buyer may be allowed to take over your mortgage, even if your original loan documents state it is non-assumable.

- **Deed-in-Lieu of Foreclosure:** As a last resort, you "give back" your property and the debt is forgiven. This will not save your house, but it is less damaging to your credit rating. This option might sound like the easiest way out, but it has limitations:

  - ✓ You usually have to try to sell the home for its fair market value for at least ninety days before the lender will consider this option.
  - ✓ This option may not be available if you have other liens such as other creditor

judgments, second mortgages, and/or tax liens.

Resources for Finding a Real Estate Agent and Selling Your Home: If you need to sell your home, you'll have to answer many questions. You'll need to find how much your house is actually worth, and you'll have to find a real estate agent you are comfortable with. The following resources may help:

- The National Association of Realtors: ***www.realtor.org/***
- The National Association of Real Estate Brokers: ***www.nareb.com/***
- The National Association of Hispanic Real Estate Professionals: ***www.nahrep.org/***
- The International Real Estate Digest: ***www.ired.com/buymyself/canale/art3.html***

If You Have an FHA-Insured Loan and Your Lender is Not Responsive: Your lender has to follow FHA servicing guidelines and regulations for FHA-insured loans. If your lender is not cooperative, contact FHA's National Servicing Center toll free at **(888) 297-8685** or via email at

hsg-lossmit@hud.gov. HUD does *not* oversee VA or conventional loans.

> **"Predatory" lenders ... engage in lending practices which increase the chances a borrower will lose a home ..."**

Beware of Predatory Lending Schemes: Most mortgage lenders are trustworthy and provide a valuable service by allowing families to own a home without saving enough money to buy it outright, but dishonest or "predatory" lenders do exist and engage in lending practices which increase the chances a borrower will lose a home to foreclosure. Beware *especially* of those who make high risk second mortgages. Other abusive practices include:

- Making a mortgage loan to an individual who does not have the income to repay it.
- Charging excessive interest, points and fees.
- Repeatedly refinancing a loan without providing any real value to the borrower.

Borrowers facing unemployment and/or foreclosure are often targets of predatory lenders because they are desperate to find any "solution." Homeowners receive many refinancing offers in the mail which say they are "pre-approved" for credit based on the equity in their homes. Borrowing against your house may seem attractive when you are struggling to pay your mortgage and other bills, but stop and think about this: if you can't make your current payments, increasing your debt will make it *harder* to keep your home, even if you do get some temporary cash.

Beware of Scams: The world is full of unscrupulous people, and the current financial climate is fertile ground for their activities. A few things you should be aware of:

- **Equity Skimming:** In this type of scam a "buyer" approaches you offering to repay the mortgage or sell the property if you sign over the deed and move out - usually leaving you with the debt and no house. Signing over your deed does not necessarily relieve you of the responsibility of paying the loan.

> **"Signing over your deed does not necessarily relieve you of the responsibility of paying the loan."**

- **Phony Counseling Agencies** who charge for counseling which is often free of charge. If you have any doubt about paying for such services, call a HUD-approved agency.

- Do not sign anything you do not understand. It is your right and duty to ask questions!

- Call toll free at **(800) 569-4287** or TDD **(800) 877-8339** before you pay anyone or sign anything.

- Information is your best defense against becoming a victim of predatory lending, especially as a desperate homeowner.

Where to Report Suspected Predatory Lending: Homeowners can either visit the Stop Mortgage Fraud) www.stopmortgagefraud.com/) website or call toll free **(800) 348-3931** to get information on what steps to take to file a complaint. Homeowners who call will also receive a booklet containing information found on the website.

For more information about predatory lending go to:

- Freddie MAC's Predatory Lending Webpage:

www.freddiemac.com/corporate/buyown/english/mortgages/lenders/avoiding_predlend.html

- Freddie MAC's "Don't Borrow Trouble" Site:

www.dontborrowtrouble.com/

REBUILDING YOUR CREDIT AFTER FORECLOSURE

"Failure is only the opportunity to begin again more intelligently."

- Henry Ford

REBUILDING YOUR CREDIT AFTER FORECLOSURE

First and foremost, there is no "magic bullet" with respect to rebuilding your credit after foreclosure. The damage has been done to your credit, typically all along the way to the final action being taken by the mortgage company. In most cases there are likely to be unpaid credit card bills, as well as late payments on the car, utilities or other obligations. The actions you take at this point will determine how long it will take to get back on your feet and re-establish yourself so you may be able to purchase another house in the future - if that is what you and your family want to do.

"... There is no 'magic bullet' with respect to rebuilding your credit ..."

Your first action should be to review your credit reports and take an assessment of your situation. Be honest with yourself, and remember this is not the time to become discouraged because of what has happened. Some of the realities you must confront:

- Depending on whether you have a deficiency judgment to address, you must begin to make arrangements to bring accounts to a current state.

    - If you have had a judgment filed against you, this may cause long term difficulty and tax liability. You should start paying it as soon as possible. This could easily be the largest balance due. At the very least this is a judgment and should take priority over all other obligations because this, even if all other items are clear, is the *only* one which may attach to any new house you seek to purchase. Sometimes you can negotiate a lower payoff, especially if you are able to pay the new amount agreed upon in full.

    - If there is a shortfall in the amount the mortgage company was able to take from the sale, they will most likely report the difference to the IRS on a 1099 as income you earned and have not paid taxes on. The tax due will be based on the amount of actual difference, and your tax bracket. You should consult with a tax professional to better determine what the monetary damage to you will be. At the time of this writing there is legislation pending which will remove this penalty.

- Contact the creditors you have not paid and make arrangements to get back on track. You may begin by paying the smallest balance due so that you can experience some success. Call the creditor and make arrangements to pay the debt. If you can pay the amount due in full do so, if not arrange to make monthly payments. This will begin to move you towards getting your credit back on track. Remember, it takes both time and money to resolve any credit issue.

  While you are making payments on the first issue, begin to make a plan to address the next item if you have one. You may want to begin saving money for the next item by writing a letter to the creditor stating your desire to enter into an agreement to repay the debt. You should request the creditor send the new agreement for repayment to you in writing. The creditor wants to receive payment, and should not object to sending this confirmation if they are ethical. Remember your credit has simply taken a step backward and yes, you *can* rebuild it. It will take time and patience. Keep copies of all checks or money orders used for payments. Maintain careful records of what monies you send, and documentation of the outcome.

- When a debt is paid off write a letter to all three Credit Reporting Agencies - *Equifax*, *Transunion* and *Experion*. When you send your letter include a copy of the canceled bank check or money order. A bank check is preferred because you will have a copy of the canceled check as proof of payment. You may also be able to get the creditor to include the statement "paid as agreed" or "paid as per agreement." If you enter into payment arrangements keep track of the payments made and ask if they will be reported to the credit reporting agencies. Another reason bank checks are preferred is because if the creditor won't report payments to the credit agencies you will have proof of the amounts and dates they were made. You can then submit a copy of the letter from the creditor agreeing to payment arrangements along with copies of the cancelled checks to the credit agencies yourself to see if they will investigate on their own and subsequently update your credit record. This is a long shot, but if you are able to get it done it certainly helps. Your objective is to have your payments placed on the record to show your good faith and willingness to make an effort to get back on your feet.

- Once you have begun to repay any outstanding debts you can begin the process of reestablishing your credit. One way to do this is to go to your Bank, Savings and Loan Association or Credit Union and ask if they would be willing to give you a secured credit card. A secured card will allow you to rebuild credit and have that information reported to the credit reporting agencies. With a secured credit card you are, in effect, pledging money as collateral against the card. The lender may allow you to use the full amount of the deposit or a large percentage of the funds.

  When you have enough funds to obtain another secured card from a different company you should do so. It is imperative for you to *use the card* and *repay the balance as quickly as possible.* Remember that you are working on rebuilding your credit, and the cards should be used with great discretion. Creating two lines of credit places you on track to purchasing a home again after approximately twenty-four months.

What you have done is provide proof positive you are willing and able to manage your credit properly. By paying your bills on time, you demonstrate to future creditors you are making a concerted effort to rebuild your credit. Your actions are reported to the credit bureaus, and will have a positive impact on your credit history and score.

"Using so-called "Credit Repair Companies" offering to remove any and all bad credit from your record could constitute FRAUD on both your part and theirs."

Rebuilding your credit will take time, and does *not* require you to pay someone to "clean up your credit." In fact, it may be illegal for them to do so. The Federal Trade Commission and possibly your state laws may deem it illegal for anyone to make an effort to "clean up your credit." Using so-called "Credit Repair Companies" offering to remove any and all bad credit from your record could constitute FRAUD on both your part and theirs. In Florida, for example, the state statute pertaining to fraud clearly states if someone makes a false statement regarding their credit it is illegal.

In other words, beware of those signs on the side of road proclaiming how they will eradicate all your bad credit including foreclosure, judgments, collections, etc. The truth is if the item in your credit was reported correctly and factually, they *cannot* simply erase the bad history. Only time and money will cure bad credit.

The only person who can repair your credit is *you*. To believe someone else can do it *for* you is to potentially place yourself into a position of being used and hurt. Ignorance is not an excuse. You may want to discuss your situation with a credit counselor. In fact the HUD housing counselor you may have spoken with when you were having credit difficulty with your house may be able to help, or at the very least refer you to someone who can.

Accurate Negative Credit Information Cannot be Erased: If a credit repair company tells you it will be able to remove negative information from your credit report, they may not be telling the truth. Accurate information which is within seven years of the date the credit report is pulled, or ten years if the information relates to a bankruptcy, *cannot* be erased from a credit report. The only information which can be changed are items which are actually wrong, or are beyond the seven or ten year reporting period.

Hiding Bad Credit May Be Illegal: Some credit repair schemes promise you they can "hide" bad credit by helping you establish a new credit identity. If you pay a fee for such a service the company may direct you to apply for an Employer Identification Number (EIN) from the Internal Revenue Service, and to use the EIN in place of your social security number when you apply for credit. You may also be instructed to use a new mailing address. This practice, known as *file segregation*, is a federal crime!

How to Protect Yourself: Restoring your credit is a time consuming process and must be undertaken with clear understanding and planning. Once you have begun to reestablish your credit you must show new creditors you can be trusted with their money once again. This will not be easy. One of the things you must avoid is the temptation to take shortcuts in the reestablishment of your credit. You will receive many solicitations for credit cards, and applications for new loans and various types of credit - all of which appear to be easy to obtain. When you receive such an offer do yourself a favor and ignore it. There is a good reason for ignoring the so called "Credit Rebuilding Programs" offered by any number of sub-prime credit card companies.

"You were successful once, and you can be again!"

These companies don't have the desire to help you restore your credit they claim to. Their words on paper sound 'oh so sweet,' and they will make claims which sound simply fantastic. Read the offers carefully, especially the fine print and grey text most of us tend to ignore. Read the terms and conditions carefully, paying particular attention to the area devoted to the "cost of money." Study and understand the rate, most particularly if it is variable - as most of these types of credit cards tend to be. The rate will generally be higher than what you were able to qualify for before, but as previously mentioned if you have taken out a secured card from your bank or credit union you won't need what these companies are offering.

If you have done everything you should, such as finding suitable housing and paying your rent and utilities on time and making sure all of your normal obligations have been paid as required, you are well on your way to being back to normal. Remember, now is *not* the time to become discouraged. Keep faith that you can overcome this crisis, and do what is required. Although it may sometimes seem to be impossible, it really isn't. If you want it bad enough you can achieve it. You were successful once, and you can be again!"

WHAT DOES THE FUTURE HOLD?

"The difference between stumbling blocks and stepping stones is the way a man uses them."

- From a Motivational Poster

> **"...you can rebuild and start over - this time probably a little wiser..."**

If you have been able to save your home through a workout agreement with your lender the next few months and years will be crucial. You have probably sacrificed a lot to keep your home, and you will continue to have to do so. You *must* make sure all your payments are on time and start rebuilding your credit as soon as possible. In time, with patience and determination, you can begin to minimize the effects of your recent negative credit situation. Utilizing some of the ideas discussed in the previous chapter may be helpful, but most importantly build and maintain a relationship with your housing counselors and seek their guidance.

If you have lost your home either through foreclosure, short sale, or some other method, this does not mean it is the end of the world. Although you have just come through a very stressful and devastating time, you can rebuild and start over - this time probably a little wiser and more aware of the proper steps to take and choices to make. For most, renting will be a way of life for a while. Renting has a lot of positive aspects for someone who has just lost their house. It can be a time for healing, and is much less stressful. When renting, if something breaks, you just call your landlord. No worries about unexpected repair bills and escalating insurance and taxes. Let someone else worry about those things for awhile!

You will have a lot more free time on your hands. Use that time to do something nice for you and your family. Do things that don't take a lot of money, but can improve your mental health and quality of life. Pack a lunch, go to a park or the beach, take a deep breath, and exhale.

Once you have had time to heal, you may want to take the steps necessary to buy a home again. This time you'll be a little wiser and much more knowledgeable. No matter what caused you to lose your home, whether it was loss of income, illness, or not having the required understanding of the type of loan program you were given, you *can* own a home again - if you choose.

Although you may not be able to plan for every possible condition which can lead to foreclosure, it is our hope this book you will give you a good idea of the right way to go about the business of homeownership. It is a very serious commitment which can have devastating consequences on homeowners who have not been properly educated in the home buying process and don't have the proper grasp of their responsibilities or a clear understanding of the mortgage they are getting.

We also hope you understand that not everyone has your best interests at heart. There are those who, for their own personal financial benefit, exploit the desire of potential homeowners to own a piece of the American Dream. The next time you will not be so quick to take at face value what you are told. You will do your own research and investigating. If you don't feel adequately prepared to take on the task of reviewing documentation, sifting through a myriad of lenders, and choosing the best priced home and mortgage loan for you, you now know there are resources available to hold your hand and guide you every step of the way. Why not take advantage of their services?

It is imperative for you to check HUD's website for the most up-to-date listings. Never take anything for granted. Do your own research, and/or get the help of someone who can guide you through your next home buying adventure.

Sometimes, if handled properly, tough times can serve to galvanize a family and make them closer - especially if all family members are involved in the process. If it is your choice to be a renter that's okay, but in the future you may change your mind. Don't let the negative experience you have just come through deter you from ever wanting to buy a home again. It really can be a wonderful experience to have a place to call home where you can create good and happy memories.

It is our hope that this book has been instrumental in helping guide you through the complicated maze of foreclosure and homeownership retention. Make sure you take advantage of the resources available and now, with a better understanding of the process, go forward in confidence and take care of the task ahead. We wish you the best in finding the right outcome for you . . . .

FREQUENTLY ASKED QUESTIONS

"Perhaps the most valuable result of all education and knowledge is the ability to make ourselves do the thing we have to do when it ought to be done, whether we like it or not."

- Thomas H. Huxley

Q: What happens when I miss my mortgage payments?

A: Foreclosure may occur, which means your lender can legally repossess your home. When this happens, you must move out of your house. If your property is worth less than the total amount you owe on your mortgage a deficiency judgment could be pursued, meaning in addition to losing your home you would owe HUD or your lender money. Both foreclosures and deficiency judgments could seriously affect your ability to qualify for credit in the future, so avoid foreclosure if at all possible.

What should I do?

- *Do not ignore letters* from your lender. If you are having problems making your payments, call or write to your lender's loss mitigation department immediately. Explain your situation, and be prepared to provide financial information such as your monthly income and expenses. Without this information, they may not be able to help.

- Stay in your home for now. You may not qualify for assistance if you abandon your property.

- Contact a HUD-approved foreclosure housing counseling agency. Call toll free **1-800-569-4287** or TDD **(800) 877-8339** for the housing counseling agency nearest you. These agencies are valuable resources. They have information on services and programs offered by government agencies and private and community organizations that might be able to help you. The housing counseling agency may also offer credit counseling. These services are usually free of charge.

Q: Who is my lender? How do I make contact?

A: Look at your monthly mortgage coupons or billing statements for the lender's name and contact information.

Q: I don't remember what type of mortgage I have. How can I find this information?

A: Look on the original mortgage documents or call your mortgage lender.

Q: Do I need to keep living in my house to qualify for assistance?

A: Usually yes, but call your lender to discuss your specific circumstances and get advice on options which may be available.

Q: When can a lender foreclose?

A: To exercise a foreclosure against a borrower's property, the lender(s) must follow certain statutory procedures set forth in statute, local laws, or mortgage documents. A lender can begin a foreclosure when a borrower defaults under the terms, covenants and conditions contained in the Note and/or Deed of Trust and as governed by state law. Most often a foreclosure is begun because a borrower has not paid one or more of their regular installment payments. Default occurs after one missed payment, but the foreclosure process typically would not begin until the default period has gone to three or more missed payments.

Q: How can a lender try to collect from a borrower?

A: The Lender may begin following up with borrowers if their payments are not received by the due date, which in most cases is the first day of the month. The first contact is attempted by telephone, with a follow up letter. If the borrower fails to respond to both telephone and/or written notice of the late payment, the lender will send a letter letting them know of the lender's intention to foreclose. The lender/creditor is bound to follow the Fair Debt Collection Practices Act ("FDCPA") when collecting a debt. If the lender violates this FDCPA, they can be subject to large penalties.

Q: What are the costs associated with a foreclosure?

A: The lender may use a specialist company to provide foreclosure services, from filing *the Notice of Default* through conducting the *Trustee's Sale*.
Acting as the Trustee, the company may charge fees as allowed by law. In addition the Trustee passes along mailing, postal, recording, legal and other related costs and expenses connected with the foreclosure. Some additional expenses might be inspection and property security costs. The trustee purchases a *Trustee's Sale Guaranty* from a title company and publishes a required *Notice of Sale* in local newspapers or other publications located near the property, resulting in additional costs and expenses. Publishing and postal fees will vary, depending upon where the property is located, where the notice is placed (the actual publication) and the length of the legal description of the property.

Q: Who pays for the foreclosure?

A: If the borrower reinstates the loan, pays off the loan during foreclosure, or enters into a *Forbearance Agreement*, the foreclosure fees, costs and expenses are collected from the borrower. Once the Final Judgment of Foreclosure is entered by the Judge, the costs associated with the foreclosure action are incorporated in the total amount of the judgment. At the time of the sale, the lender is provided a full credit in the amount of the judgment plus interest from the date the judgment was entered. Therefore, if the property sells to a third party at the foreclosure sale, the lender recoups the foreclosure expenses from the third party funds. If the lender does not recoup all of the money owed to them through the foreclosure process, the lender may seek additional relief by filing a Deficiency action. In a Deficiency action the lender is seeking a judgment against you personally for the remaining amount due and owing to the lender, unlike the foreclosure action where the lender is seeking to recoup their money by the forced sale of the property you own.

Q: My employer has already announced layoffs for the coming month. What can I do now?

A: You have started learning about available options here. Now, figure out if a layoff will make it hard for your family to make your mortgage payments. If so, consider other resources you have to pay your mortgage. Review your spending habits and see where you can reduce spending. If you have a lot of other debt, consider contacting a nonprofit consumer credit counseling agency. Take advantage of any help your employer offers. If you still believe you will have trouble making your mortgage payments, contact your lender right away.

Q: What are the key points to remember?

1. Don't lose your home and damage your credit history.

2. Call or write your mortgage lender *immediately* and be *honest* about your financial situation.

3. Stay in your home to make sure you qualify for assistance.

4. Arrange an appointment with a HUD-approved housing counselor at to explore your options toll free at **(800) 569-4287** or TDD **(800) 877-8339.**

5. Cooperate with the counselor or lender who is trying to help you.

6. Explore *every* alternative to keep your home.

7. Beware of scams.

8. Never sign anything you don't understand. Remember, signing over the deed to someone else does not necessarily relieve you of your loan obligation.

9. Act *now!* Delaying can't help. If you do nothing you will lose your home and your good credit rating.

Q: What precautions can I take?

A: These precautions can help you avoid being "taken" by a scam artist:

- Don't sign any papers you don't fully understand.
- Make sure you get all "promises" in writing.
- Beware of any sales contract that assumes the loan but in which you are not *formally* released from liability (responsibility) for your mortgage debt.
- Check with a lawyer or your mortgage company before entering into any deal involving your home.

If you're selling the house yourself to avoid foreclosure, check to see if there are any complaints against the prospective buyer. You can contact your state's Attorney General, State Real Estate Commission, or the local District Attorney's Consumer Fraud Unit for this type of information.

Q: Will I be responsible for any out-of-pocket expenses if I am approved for a workout option?

A: You may have to pay expenses such as recording fees for a loan modification. Because every situation is different, contact your lender for more information. But, if a lender has no contact with you and has to start foreclosure, you may have to pay very high legal fees. To avoid this, call your lender as soon as you realize you might have trouble.

SERVICE MEMBERS CIVIL RELIEF ACT (SCRA) QUESTIONS: Reservists, guardsmen and other military personnel can find answers to questions about mortgage payment relief and protection from foreclosure provided by the Service Members Civil Relief Act of 2003 (formerly The Soldiers' and Sailors' Civil Relief Act of 1940).

Q: Who is eligible?

A: The Act applies to active duty military personnel who had a mortgage obligation before enlistment or before being ordered to active duty. This includes:

- Members of the Army, Navy, Marine Corps, Air Force, Coast Guard.

- Commissioned officers of the Public Health Service and the National Oceanic and Atmospheric Administration engaged in active service.

- Reservists ordered to report for military service.

- People ordered to report for induction (training) under the Military Selective Service Act.

- Guardsmen called to active service for more than thirty consecutive days.

- In limited situations, dependents of service members are also entitled to protections.

Q: Am I entitled to debt payment relief?

A: The Act limits the interest which may be charged on mortgages taken out by a service member (including debts incurred jointly with a spouse) before he or she entered into active military service. At your request, lenders must reduce the interest rate to no more than 6% per year during the period of active military service and recalculate your payments to reflect the lower rate. This provision applies to both conventional and government-insured mortgages.

Q: Is the interest rate limitation automatic?

A: No. To get this temporary interest rate reduction you must submit a written request to your mortgage lender and include a copy of your military orders. The request may be submitted as soon as the orders are issued, but no later than 180 days after the date of your release from active duty military service.

Q: Am I eligible even if I can afford to pay my mortgage at a higher interest rate?

A: If a mortgage lender believes military service has not affected your ability to repay your mortgage, they have the right to ask a court to grant relief from the interest rate reduction. This is does not happen very often.

Q: What if I can't afford to pay my mortgage even at the lower rate?

A: Your mortgage lender may let you stop paying the principal amount due on your loan during active duty service. Lenders are not *required* to do this, but they generally try to work with service members to help keep them in their homes. You will still owe this amount, but will not have to repay it until after you complete active duty service.

Most lenders have other programs to assist borrowers who can't make their mortgage payments. If you or your spouse finds yourself in this position at any time before or after active duty service, contact your lender immediately and ask about loss mitigation options. If you have an FHA-insured loan and are having difficulty making mortgage payments, you may also be eligible for special forbearance and other loss mitigation options.

Q: Am I protected against foreclosure?

A: Mortgage lenders may not foreclose while you are on active duty or within a ninety day period after military service without court approval. A lender would be required to show the court your ability to repay the debt was not affected by military service.

Q: What information do I need to provide to my lender?

A: When you or your representative contacts your mortgage lender, you should provide the following information:

- Notice that you have been called to active duty.

- A copy of the orders from the military notifying you of your activation.
- Your FHA case number or loan number.
- Evidence that the debt precedes your activation date.

HUD has reminded FHA lenders of their obligation to follow the SCRA. When notified that a borrower is on active military duty, an FHA lender must inform the borrower or representative of the adjusted payment amount due, provide adjusted coupons or billings, and ensure adjusted payments are not considered insufficient payments.

Q: Will my payments change later, and will I need to pay back the interest rate "subsidy" at a later date?

A: The change in interest rate is not a subsidy. Interest in excess of 6% per year which would otherwise have been charged is forgiven, however the reduction in the interest rate and monthly payment amount only applies during the period of active duty. Once the period of active military service ends, the interest rate will revert back to the original interest rate and payments will be recalculated accordingly.

Q: How long does the benefit last? Does the period begin and end with my tour of duty?

A: Interest rate reductions are only for the period of active military service. Other benefits, such as postponement of monthly principal payments on the loan and restrictions on foreclosure, may begin immediately upon assignment to active military service and end on the third month following the term of active duty assignment.

Q: How can I learn more about relief available to active duty military personnel?

A: Service Members who have questions about the SCRA or the protections they may be entitled to can contact their unit judge advocate or installation legal assistance officer. Dependents of service members can also contact or visit local military legal assistance offices where they live. A military legal assistance office locator for each branch of the armed forces is available at:

www.legalassistance.law.af.mil/content/locator.php

This is a general guide only. Laws change, and you need to check your state statutes for accurate, up to date procedures. Foreclosure type will most often be either judicial or non-judicial. Deficiency Judgments are available in some states if the lender loses money through the foreclosure process. Homeowner redemption after foreclosure is possible in some states, and the time periods are listed where available.

RESOURCE GUIDE

"Success . . . seems to be connected with action. Successful men keep moving. They make mistakes, but they don't quit."

- Conrad Hilton

MORTGAGE LENDERS

The mortgage lenders listed in the table on the facing page have voluntarily joined the federal government to assist homeowners who are concerned about the future or have suffered due to recent changes in the economy. If your lender is listed here, you can help protect your home by contacting them immediately!

Lender	Phone #1	Phone #2
Bank of America	(800) 846-2222	(716) 635-2264
Chase Home Finance	(800) 848-9136	
Chase Home Finance	(800) 526-0072 ext. 533	(800) 527-3040
CitiMortgage	(800) 926-9783	
Countrywide	(800) 763-1255	(800) 669-4576
HSBC Mortgage Corporation	(800) 338-6441	(888) 648-3124
Irwin Mortgage Corporation	(888) 444-6446	
James B. Nutter & Company	(800) 315-7334	
Midland Mortgage	(800) 552-3000	(800) 654-4566
Mortgage Service	(800) 449-8767	
National City Mortgage	(800) 367-9305	
Principal Residential Mortgage, Inc.	(800) 367-6448	(800) 962-4450
Wells Fargo Mortgage	(800) 766-0987	
Wendover Financial Services Corporation	(888) 934-1081	(800) 436-1022
Washington Mutual Home Loans, Inc.	(866) 926-8937	(800) 254-3677

TYPES OF FORECLOSURE BY STATE

Following is an alphabetical listing by state outlining the appropriate type of foreclosure, months to foreclosure, whether a deficiency judgment is possible, practical or not and what, if any, is the redemption period in your state.

STATE	TYPE OF FORECLOSURE	MONTHS TO FORECLOSURE	DEFICENCY JUDGMENT	REDEDMPTION PERIOD
ALABAMA	PRIMARILY NON-JUDICIAL	1-3	POSSIBLE & PRACTICAL	12
ALASKA	BOTH	3-4	NOT PRACTICAL	NONE
ARIZONA	BOTH	3-4	NOT PRACTICAL	NONE
ARKANSAS	BOTH	4-5	POSSIBLE & PRACTICAL	NONE
CALIFORNIA	PRIMARILY NON-JUDICIAL	4-4	NOT PRACTICAL	NONE
COLORADO	BOTH	2-5	POSSIBLE & PRACTICAL	75 DAYS
CONNECTICUT	JUDICAL STRICT	5-6	POSSIBLE & PRACTICAL	75 DAYS
DELAWARE	JUDICAL	3-7	POSSIBLE & PRACTICAL	NONE
DISTRICT OF COLUMBIA	NON-JUDICIAL	2-4	POSSIBLE & PRACTICAL	NONE
FLORIDA	JUDICIAL	5-5	POSSIBLE &	NONE

			PRACTICAL	
GEORGIA	PRIMARILY NON-JUDICIAL	2-2	POSSIBLE & PRACTICAL	NONE
HAWAII	PRIMARILY NON-JUDICIAL	3-4	NOT PRACTICAL	NONE
IDAHO	NON-JUDCIAL	5-6	POSSIBLE & PRACTICAL	NONE
ILLINOIS	JUDICIAL	7-10	POSSIBLE & PRACTICAL	NONE
INDIANA	JUDICIAL	5-7	POSSIBLE & PRACTICAL	3 MONTHS
IOWA	BOTH	5-6	NOT PRACTICAL IF JUDICIAL	6 MONTHS
KANSAS	JUDICIAL	4-4	POSSIBLE & PRACTICAL	6-12 MONTHS
KENTUCY	JUDICIAL	6-5	POSSIBLE & PRACTICAL	NONE
LOUISIANA	JUDICIAL	2-6	POSSIBLE & PRACTICAL	NONE
MAINE	PRIMARILY JUDICIAL	6-10	POSSIBLE & PRACTICAL	NONE
MARYLAND	JUDICIAL	2-2	POSSIBLE & PRACTICAL	NONE
MASSACHUSETTS	NON-JUDICIAL	3-4	POSSIBLE & PRACTICAL	NONE
MICHIGAN	BOTH	2-2	POSSIBLE & PRACTICAL	6 MONTHS
MINNESOTA	BOTH	2-3	NOT PRACTICAL	6 MONTHS

MISSISSIPPI	PRIMARILY NON-JUDICIAL	2-3	POSSIBLE & PRACTICAL	NONE
MISSOURI	PRIMARILY NON-JUDICIAL	2-2	POSSIBLE PRACTICAL	NONE
MONTANA	PRIMARILY NON-JUDICIAL	5-5	NOT PRACTICAL	NONE
NEBRASKA	JUDICIAL	5-6	POSSIBLE & PRACTICAL	NONE
NEVADA	PRIMARILY NON-JUDICIAL	4-4	POSSIBLE & PRACTICAL	NONE
NEW HAMPSHIRE	PRIMARILY NON-JUDICIAL	2-3	POSSIBLE & PRACTICAL	NONE
NEW JERSEY	JUDICIAL	3-10	POSSIBLE & PRACTICAL	10 DAYS
NEW MEXICO	JUDICIAL	4-6	POSSIBLE & PRACTICAL	NONE
NEW YORK	JUDICIAL	4-8	POSSIBLE & PRACTICAL	NONE
NORTH CAROLINA	NON-JUDICIAL	2-4	POSSIBLE & PRACTICAL	NONE
NORTH DAKOTA	JUDICIAL	3-5	NOT POSSIBLE	60 DAYS
OHIO	JUDICIAL	5-7	POSSIBLE & PRACTICAL	NONE
OKLAHOMA	PRIMARILY JUDICIAL	4-7	POSSIBLE & PRACTICAL	NONE
OREGON	BOTH		POSSIBLE & PRACTICAL	YES
PENNSYLVANIA	JUDICIAL	3-9	NOT PRACTICAL	NONE

RHODE ISLAND	BOTH	2-3	POSSIBLE & PRACTICAL	NONE
SOUTH CAROLINA	JUDICIAL	6-6	NOT PRACTICAL	NONE
SOUTH DAKOTA	BOTH		POSSIBLE & PRACTICAL	YES
TENNESSEE	NON-JUDICIAL	2-2	POSSIBLE & PRACTICAL	NONE
TEXAS	NON-JUDICIAL	2-2	POSSIBLE & PRACTICAL	NONE
UTAH	BOTH	4-5	POSSIBLE & PRACTICAL	NONE
VERMONT	BOTH	7-10	POSSIBLE & PRACTICAL	NONE
VIRGIN1A	NON-JUDICIAL	2-2	POSSIBLE & PRACTICAL	NONE
WASHINGTON	NON-JUDICIAL	4-5	NOT PRACTICAL	NONE
WEST VIRGINIA	NON-JUDICIAL	2-2	POSSIBLE & PRACTICAL	NONE
WISCONSIN	JUDICIAL	VARIES-10	NOT PRACTICAL	NONE
WYOMING	NON-JUDICIAL	2-3	POSSIBLE & PRACTICAL	3 MONTHS

Federal Housing Administration (FHA)

FHA is the *Federal Housing Administration* which is often referred to as HUD (The U. S. Department of Housing and Urban Development), and is for all intents and purposes an insurance company which offers insurance and assurance to lenders so that if your mortgage were to go into default there would be some financial relief. As a result lenders are more willing to make loans which may carry slightly more risk than the regular market is willing to take. FHA may offer more options to the borrower as remedies to keep the house than they may be aware of, so it is highly recommended the borrower contact FHA for further guidance.

www.FHA.gov

Neighborworks

Neighborworks is a major national not-for-profit which primarily provides support and training to other not-for-profit agencies across the United States. As it relates to the pre-foreclosure and counseling processes, look for agencies which are affiliated with and/or have been trained and certified by Neighborworks as this is an assurance you are working with an agency with the highest level of training. HEA is an Affiliate of Neighborworks through our primary affiliation with NCLR.

www.Neighborworks.org

Neighborhood Housing Services of America

Second to Neighborworks is *Neighborhood Housing Services of America*. They also provide national support and training to local not-for-profits, and ensure affiliated agencies adhere to the highest standards.

www.nhsaonline.org

Nation Council of La Raza

Nation Council of La Raza is a national not-for-profit which supports other smaller not-for-profit agencies across the United States. NCLR has local affiliates who speak both Spanish and English with a focus on the Latino Community, and is often perceived as being a culturally sensitive agency network for those who speak Spanish as a primary language. HEA is a *La Raza* affiliate.

www.nclr.org

The National Association of Hispanic Real Estate Professionals (NAHREP)

A non-profit 501c6 trade association with 15,000 members in over 60 affiliate chapters in 48 states. Based in Washington, D.C., the members are real estate agents, brokers, loan officers, mortgage brokers, title officers, escrow officers, appraisers, insurance agents and more. They are from diverse cultural backgrounds, as membership is not limited to professionals of Hispanic descent. NAHREP's mission is to increase Hispanic homeownership rates by empowering the advisors that serve them through educational tools, a networking forum, and the power of advocacy.

www.nahrep.org

Federal Home Loan Mortgage Corporation (FHLMC)

Freddie Mac is essentially the same as FannieMae except they are not backed by the Federal Government and they are direct competitors. As with Fannie Mae you must meet the lending guidelines as established by FreddieMac, and they may be in a position to help you in the event all other remedies have been exhausted. There are only a few situations where Freddie would be willing to intervene directly, so you should not rely on them for help. Conventional Conforming Mortgages are in some cases Freddie Mac Mortgages.

www.Freddiemac.com

Federal National Mortgage Association (FNMA)

Fannie Mae is the company which may own your mortgage and acts a "Broker" with regard to the buying and selling of your mortgage over its life. You had to meet the lending requirements of FannieMae before you were approved for your mortgage, and they may still be able to help in a worst case scenario. There are only a few situations where Fannie would be willing to directly intervene so you should not rely on them for direct help. Conventional Conforming Mortgages are in some cases Fannie Mae Mortgages.

www.Fanniemae.org

Home Free USA

Home Free USA is a smaller largely regional to near national agency with affiliates scattered across the United States. They provide support and offer affiliation through Neighborworks for their network of agencies.

www.homefree.org

Veteran's Administration (VA)

A VA loan is a mortgage loan in the United States guaranteed by the Veterans Administration. In order to obtain a VA mortgage you must be a qualified Veteran. One of the benefits is the VA guarantees the loan to the lender, as compared to the other loan types such as Fannie or Freddie conventional mortgages. Veterans have a great many protections through the VA, so it is recommended they contact them if in mortgage default.

www.VA.gov

BankRate

BankRate.com is a website where you can find very good information on banking, mortgages, and finance. There are, for instance, calculators you can use to see what a monthly payment would be if a particular interest rate or term is used. Various "what if" scenarios can be run as well, so you can know what to do in different situations and be prepared to make good decisions.

www.bankrate.com

Federal Trade Commission

Contains clear and easy to read consumer rights regarding issues of credit, banking, mortgages etc. This information is provided by the Federal Government and is highly recommended as a source.

www.FTC.gov

Annual Credit Report.com

This central site allowS you to request a free credit file disclosure, commonly called a credit report, once every 12 months from each of the nationwide consumer credit reporting companies: Equifax, Experian and TransUnion.

www.annualcreditreport.com

About.com

This site features introductory articles on a wide variety of subjects including mortgages and credit.

www.about.com

All of us are paid for the work we do, and the frequency of that payment may vary from weekly to monthly to other situations where being paid may depend on sales or production, in other words you may be paid from the proceeds of your small business. Whatever the frequency of your payment there is relatively simple way to compute your monthly gross income. Remember this is how you were initially pre-qualified by your lender and it is how the Mortgage Company will determine your eligibility to qualify for one of the "Work Out Options" or "Loss Mitigation Options" which may offered by the Mortgage Company. The following are some simple examples to use in computing your gross monthly income.

If you are paid:

By the hour $________ x _______ x 52 weeks ÷ 12 months = $ _______
Pay before deductions X # hours worked Gross monthly income

Weekly $ __________ x52 weeks ÷ 12 months = $ __________
Pay before deductions Gross monthly income

Bi-weekly $ __________ x 26 ÷ 12 months = $ __________
Pay before deductions Gross monthly income

Twice a month $ __________ x24 ÷ 12 months = $ __________
Pay before deductions Gross monthly income

Once a month $ __________ $ __________
Gross monthly income

Not regularly $ __________ ÷ 12 months = $ __________
Income from last year's tax return before deductions Gross monthly income

Other gross monthly income included from co-borrower's or other gross monthly derived from any other sources $ __________

Total Gross Monthly Income $ __________

Total Monthly Debt Worksheet

From your monthly budget list the debts you currently pay

Your total monthly debt payments

Mortgage payment $ __________

Automobile payment $ __________

Credit Cards Minimum monthly payment

______________________________ $ __________

______________________________ $ __________

______________________________ $ __________

______________________________ $ __________

______________________________ $ __________

Total monthly debt from credit cards $ __________

Personal Loan Payments

__________________________ __ $ __________

____________________________ $ __________

Total monthly debt from all loans $ __________

Child support payments $ __________

Child Care $ ______________________ x 52 ÷ 12 $ __________
Weekly cost of child care

Alimony Payments $ __________

Total Monthly Debt $ __________

Mortgage Re-Qualifying Worksheet

Total gross monthly income $ _________ (1)

Total gross monthly income x _____ % $ _________ (2)
(housing ratio)

Total gross monthly income x _____ % $_________ (3)
(debt to income ration)

Total monthly debt payments $ _________ (4)

Subtract line (4) from line (3) $ _________ (5)

Maximum mortgage loan payment

Enter whichever is less, line (2) or line (5) $ _________ (6)

Divide line (6) by sample rate factor on page 205 $ _________ (7)

Add tax and insurance payments to total $ _________ (8)

Maximum mortgage loan amount $ _________ (9)

Multiply line (9) by 1,000 $ _________

Sample Interest Rate Factor

Dollars repaid per $1,000 borrowed by term:

Interest rate	15 year loan	20 year loan	30 year
5.00	$7.91	$6.60	$5.37
5.50	$8.17	$6.88	$5.68
6.00	$8.44	$7.16	$6.00
6.50	$8.71	$7.46	$6.32
7.00	$8.99	$7.75	$6.65
7.50	$9.27	$8.06	$6.99
8.00	$9.56	$8.36	$7.34
8.50	$9.85	$8.68	$7.69
9.00	$10.14	$9.00	$8.05
9.50	$10.44	$9.32	$8.41
10.00	$10.75	$9.65	$8.78
10.50	$11.05	$9.98	$9.15
11.00	$11.37	$10.32	$9.53
11.50	$11.68	$10.66	$9.91
12.00	$12.00	$11.01	$10.29

SAMPLE BUDGET

Housing

Mortgage $ _______
Heating $ _______
Electricity $ _______
Water and Sewage $ _______
Telephone(s) $_______
Homeowners insurance $ _______
Property Taxes $ _______
Trash $ _______
HOA Dues $ _______
Home maintenance and furnishing $ _______
Cleaning supplies $ _______

Transportation

Gas $ _______
Car payment $ _______
Car Insurance $ _______
Car Inspection $ _______
Car repairs and maintenance $ _______
License plates & registration fees $ _______
Public transportation or taxi $ _______
Parking & tolls $ _______

Food

Groceries $ _______
School lunches $ _______
Work-related (lunches & snacks) $ _______

Insurance

Health $ _______
(Medical & dental, if not payroll deducted)
Life $ _______
Disability $ _______

Medical
Doctor $ _______
Dentist $ _______
Prescriptions $ _______

Child Care

Child Care tuition $ _______
Child support or alimony $ _______

Clothing

Clothing $ _______
Laundry and dry cleaning $ _______
Donations $ _______

Education

Tuition/Student Loan $ _______
Books, papers, & supplies $ _______
News papers & magazines $ _______
Lessons (sports, dance, music) $ _______

Entertainment

Movies, sporting events, concerts, etc. $ _______
Video Rentals $ _______

Internet service $ _______
Restaurants & take-out meals $ _______
Cable & satellite TV $ _______
Gambling & lottery tickets $ _______
Fitness or social clubs $ _______

Debts

Student Loan(s) $ _______
Credit Card monthly total $______(minimum payments)
Medical bills $ _______
Personal Loan(s) $ _______
Other total $ _______

Vacations/trips

Hobbies or crafts $ _______
Fitness or social clubs $ _______
Vacations/trips $ _______

Gifts

Birthdays $ _______
Major Holidays $_______
Personal $ _______
Barber or beauty shop $ _______
Toiletries $ _______
Children's allowances $ _______
Tobacco products $ _______
Beer, wine or liquor $ _______

Miscellaneous

Checking account & money order fees $ _______

Pet care & supplies $ _______
Postage $ _______
Pictures & photo processing $ _______
"Mad" money $ _______
Other not included monthly expenses $ _______

Grand total recurring monthly expenses $ _______

An interactive budget from Microsoft: http://office.microsoft.com/en-us/templates/TC010233421033.aspx

Glossary

Arrears - See *Forbearance.*

Assumption - The transfer of the seller's existing mortgage to the buyer, typically requiring the buyer to purchase the seller's equity.

Balloon Loans - Loans in which regular monthly payments are followed by a lump sum payment of the total outstanding balance. Negative amortization of the loan may occur, allowing the unpaid balance to grow rather than diminish.

Bankruptcy - An alternative available to those who are going through a severe financial crisis and are no longer able to pay their debts.

Broker's Fees - The amount of money paid to the person who acts as an intermediary in securing mortgage funds.

Capitalization - The process of applying delinquent amounts to the outstanding principal balance of a mortgage.

Chapter 7 Bankruptcy - The type of bankruptcy wherein you are required to liquidate nonessential items of property in exchange for the cancellation of debt.

Chapter 13 Bankruptcy - The type of bankruptcy which allows you to keep your property, but requires repayment of at least some debts over a 3- to 5-year period.

Collateral - An object of value pledged by a borrower to a lender or servicer to secure a loan. If the borrower fails to meet loan repayment terms, the lender or servicer may take possession of the pledged asset to recover losses. The value of the property that the potential homebuyer desires to purchase is considered collateral in the mortgage application process.

Compromise Offer - The term often used when discussing VA pre-foreclosure sales. A compromise agreement allows the VA (Veterans Administration) to pay the lender or servicer the difference between the sales proceeds and the mortgage balance (but not in excess of the original guarantee) and is often appropriate when the property value is less than the loan balance.

Consumer Credit Report - See *Credit Report* or *Credit Record.*

Consumer Report - See *Credit Report* or *Credit Record.*

Court Judgment - A statement or declaration issued by a judge, based on legal principles.

Court Process - The mechanisms, procedures, and operational techniques which are followed by a tribunal to decide on an action or controversy between two or more parties.

Credit - A form of trust established between a lender or servicer and a borrower. If the lender or servicer believes that a prospective borrower has both the ability and willingness to repay money, then credit may be granted. The borrower is expected to live up to that trust and repay the lender or servicer.

Credit Counseling - Formal individual education on money management which is offered by a specialized credit organization or counseling agency.

Credit Insurance - An agreement in which a securing company is obligated, through the payment of a premium, to compensate damage or pay a sum of money after verifying that the consumer has not paid money owed by credit.

Credit Report or Credit Record - A report prepared and maintained by credit bureaus which contains information about a borrower's credit history and status. A credit report will usually show past loans, credit cards, and payment patterns, and will include notice of any collections. A lender or servicer will use a credit report to evaluate a loan applicant's credit worthiness. Also called a *Consumer Credit Report* or *Consumer Report.*

Creditor - Any person or business to whom the consumer owes money and who has the right to undertake legal action to obtain money owed.

Debt Collector - A company or individual dedicated to collecting unfulfilled payment obligations.

Debt Repayment Plan - An agreement in which the consumer is obligated to repay a loan which was in default.

Deed-in-Lieu of Foreclosure – A means of transferring a property from the borrower to the lender or servicer via a formal agreement between the lender or servicer and a delinquent borrower.

Default - The failure to make mortgage loan payments according to the terms of the loan. Usually a loan is considered delinquent if no payment is received thirty days after the due date, and in default after sixty to ninety days. The rights of the lender in a defaulted loan are written in the mortgage note and include the right to begin foreclosure proceedings. Default provisions are different if the loan is covered by a *Deed of Trust*.

Deficiency Judgment - A judgment against a borrower if the sale of pledged property at foreclosure does not bring in enough to pay the balance owed.

Delinquency - A loan in which payment has not been made by the due date. A lender or servicer may assess a late charge if payment is not made by the 15th day after the payment due date.

Entry and Possession Foreclosure - A type of foreclosure in which the lender or servicer enters onto the property and takes physical possession of it. (only used in four states.)

FHA/HUD Insured Mortgages - A mortgage insured by the Federal Housing Administration of the United States Department of Housing and Urban Development and made by an approved lender or servicer in accordance with the FHA/HUD regulations.

Forbearance - The term used when all parties agree to delay foreclosure or other legal action. The borrower promises to pay the arrearage or debt by a specified date. In some instances, the payments can be reduced or suspended for a period of time. Also referred to as a *Temporary Indulgence* or *Special Forbearance* or *Arrears*. The term is sometimes interchanged with *Repayment Plan.*

Forbearance Agreement - Special agreement between the lender or servicer and the borrower who is in default on a mortgage.

Foreclosure Process - The legal process which allows a lender or servicer to sell a mortgaged property to recover losses when the owner defaults on the loan. The phases involved in the foreclosure process depend on the type of foreclosure undertaken and on the statutes of each state.

Foreclosure Workout Specialist or Foreclosure Consultant - A person who counsels those who are at risk of foreclosure and who may negotiate with the lender or servicer and provide information and options relating to foreclosure prevention.

High-Cost Credit - A type of loan whereby the lender or servicer charges high interest rates, penalties for early payment, insurance charges, or other mechanisms to ensure repayment.

Interest Rates - A percentage of the loan money which is charged to the borrower. A home loan may entail several forms of interest.

Judicial Foreclosure - The type of foreclosure in which the lender or servicer has to file an action with the court to obtain a judicial decree authorizing the foreclosure sale. The lender or servicer must prove that there is a valid mortgage between the parties, that the borrower is in default of the mortgage, and that the proper procedure has been followed.

Legal Defense - An argument or series of arguments based on legal principles and used in a legal procedure in order to prove a point of one of the parties involved in a court action.

Lien - A claim of money against a property, wherein the value of the property is used as security in repayment of a debt. Examples include a mechanic's lien, which might be for the unpaid cost of building supplies, or a tax lien for unpaid property taxes. A lien is a defect on the title and needs to be settled before transfer of ownership. A lien release is a written report of the settlement of a lien and is recorded in the public record as evidence of payment.

Loan Servicer - The company which collects monthly mortgage payments and disperses property taxes and insurance payments. Loan servicers also monitor non-performing loans, contact delinquent borrowers, and notify insurers and investors of potential problems. Loan servicers may be the lender or a specialized company which just handles loan servicing under contract with the lender or the investor who owns the loan.

Loss Mitigation Tools - Options available to those who are facing financial problems, mortgage payment delinquencies, and possible foreclosure of their home. They consist of several types of agreements with the lender or servicer to cure the default; for example, partial release, mortgage modification, special forbearance, and pre-foreclosure sale.

Low-Cost Credit - A loan for which the lender or servicer charges low interest rates, no penalties for early payment, and either low or no insurance fees.

Mortgage Institution - A bank or financial establishment which offers mortgage financing.

Mortgage Modification - The act of changing any of the terms of a mortgage so that a borrower of a defaulted mortgage can avoid foreclosure. Also referred to as *Recasting*.

Non-Judicial Foreclosure - The type of foreclosure in which the lender or servicer is permitted to sell the mortgaged property at a foreclosure sale without filing a court action. In this type of foreclosure, the lender or servicer obtains a "power of sale" by means of a clause which is included in the mortgage or deed of trust.

Notice of Sale - Communication of a judicial or administrative resolution, made according to established formalities, by which the borrower is informed that the property will be sold to obtain the money to cover the loan.

Partial Release - A request by the borrower to the lender to release a portion of the mortgaged property from the mortgage after part of the loan has been repaid.

PITI - Stands for Principal, Interest, (property) Taxes, and Insurance - the typical components of a monthly mortgage payment with escrow.

Pre-Foreclosure Sale (PFS) - The term used when a borrower is allowed to sell the property for less than the amount owed in order to avoid foreclosure. This may also he referred to as a *Short Sale*. In cases involving a VA Mortgage, it is referred to as a *Compromise Offer*.

Recasting - See *Mortgage Modification*.

Refinancing - The process of obtaining replacement financing for a home. Refinancing is usually undertaken to obtain a lower interest rate or other more favorable mortgage terms.

Reinstatement Period - One of the phases of foreclosure, during which the borrower has the opportunity to stop the foreclosure process by paying the money which is owed to the lender or servicer.

Repayment Plan - Also known as *Arrears*. See *Forbearance*.

Secured Debt - A debt for which the creditor has collateral in the form of a mortgage, lien, or security interest in certain items of property. The creditor may seize the property (collateral) if the debtor defaults in repayment of the debt.

Seized - A property which is forcibly taken into custody by the officer assigned for such action.

Short Sale - See *Pre-Foreclosure Sale.*

Special Forbearance- See *Forbearance.*

Strict Foreclosure - A type of foreclosure allowed only in Connecticut and Vermont. The lender or servicer must go to court to obtain a court order declaring you to be in default of the mortgage. As a consequence, the title of the property shifts to the lender or servicer. The court sets a time for you to pay the debt and redeem the property.

Temporary Indulgence - See *Forbearance.*

Unsecured or Uninsured Debt - A debt which does not involve collateral.

Up-Front Charges - The fees charged to you by the lender or servicer at the time of accepting a mortgage loan. These include points, broker's fees, insurance, and other charges involved in the transaction.

VA Guaranteed Mortgage - Veterans Administration insured mortgages, available up to 100 percent of the purchase price to veterans and qualified military reservists.

Workout Agreement - The negotiated agreement which is made with the lender or servicer to address a default debt for you; these agreements may restructure a loan in order to avoid foreclosure.

APPENDIX

The National Association of Hispanic Real Estate Professionals (NAHREP) is very pleased to help bring this comprehensive resource guide, written by our respected and admired colleagues and champions of homeownership Sylvia Alvarez and Walter Walker of HEA, to the public at large. This guide is an invaluable and desperately needed tool in the battle to retain the level of homeownership achieved thus far - because the current crisis in the housing market is so large there are not enough knowledgeable people available to help all those who find themselves looking for assistance and direction. It provides the power of information needed to help people face, endure and rebuild themselves and once again attain the Dream of Homeownership.

The most important aspect of NAHREP's core mission is to increase the sustainable level of homeownership for all Americans. Since inception our member practitioners have been committed to this mission and have sought to memorialize their beliefs regarding how consumers should be treated as a way of distinguishing themselves amongst industry players. The NAHREP Code of Trust "En Confianza" reflects their beliefs, and was developed over many months and released to the public in September 2007. It is a code of trust, "un pacto de confianza" between the NAHREP Code of Trust Certified Professionals and consumers to bring both into a trusted professional relationship to achieve sustainable homeownership.

The following is the text of the Code which will provide the reader with insights into the best practices covering almost all the people who take part in the home buying process. It represents what NAHREP members consider to be the "gold" standard for serving their clients and ensuring the abundant flow of funds necessary to make sustainable homeownership possible at attractive rates.

NAHREP "Code of Trust" For the Real Estate Industry

"En Confianza"

NAHREP Members Are Committed to Fair Home Buying and Financing Practices

The following discussion guide is intended to serve as a sound foundation for NAHREP 's code of conduct. NAHREP is at a point in history where it will draw a line in the sand and take an affirmative stance for fair practices within the home buying and lending industries to benefit *all* Americans. Our members understand how valuable this effort can be to our community, and they overwhelmingly support it.

A March 2007 poll of NAHREP members affirmed that Hispanic real estate professionals are overwhelmingly in favor of setting standards which include:

- Stricter sanctions and standards to ensure Hispanic homebuyers are treated fairly and that sustainable homeownership is still achievable for Hispanic families.

- Appropriate federal or state regulated licensing and education standards for all mortgage professionals.

- A cap of 2 -3% on mortgage commissions .

- Industry changes that strike a fair and reasonable balance of responsibility between lenders, mortgage professionals and consumers.

The will exists among NAHREP members to define ourselves as *the* organization which will lead the way on industry best practices.

Preamble to NAHREP Code of Trust

John F. Kennedy once noted: "The Chinese use two brush strokes to write the word 'crisis'. One brush stroke stands for danger; the other for opportunity. In a crisis, be aware of the danger - but recognize the opportunity. "

Today homeowners, prospective buyers, lenders, realtors and everyone else involved in the real estate industry face a crisis not seen in many decades in the United States. For the Hispanic community specifically, a "perfect storm" of dropping values and shrinking availability of credit threaten to undermine the homeownership gains our community has made in the past twenty years. For some who bought homes from those who turned out to be unethical practitioners, the American Dream of homeownership may now be a nightmare. For others, credit availability is drying up and the possibility of reaching the American Dream seems further away than ever.

With this crisis indeed comes opportunity – especially an opportunity for NAHREP. What is demanded by the current lending environment is leadership, steady and firmly grounded in the conviction that we have the knowledge, skills and will to rebuild. NAHREP is poised to lead in helping the Hispanic community and all Americans see their way through this cycle of reduced home values and limited access to credit. We need only the courage to confront these current lending challenges head -on and dedicate ourselves to their ethical resolution.

Where should we begin? We must rebuild Trust. On one end of the spectrum we must rebuild the trust of the financial markets in the system's ability to produce investment grade financing opportunities which perform to stated expectations. On the other end, we must engender the trust of the consumer with real estate professionals that have the integrity to use their talents and skills to truly benefit the consumer. The fundamental building block is in the basic transaction of helping a family to search, acquire and keep a home for as long as they wish. The balance of the edifice, the financing mechanisms, guarantees, national and international securities markets, hinges on that fundamental building block.

Nothing builds trust better than integrity – integrity in achieving the end goal of growing the sustainable rate of homeownership not only for Hispanics, but for all Americans. That is the core of NAHREP's mission, and toward that end we commit ourselves to promoting the highest ethical standards and best practices in the real estate and lending industries Our members are real estate and lending professionals who will always put the customer's needs first and ensure they have everything they need to make informed decisions about their home buying experience. We will require our members to adhere to our Code of Trust when it comes to issues such as fair pricing, responsible underwriting, disclosures and fair servicing of loans We will strive to provide consumers with the best, most accurate information possible to help them make informed decisions about home buying We strive to will ensure that our members can explain this information in the clearest, simplest terms.

NAHREP members believe customers deserve to

deal with real estate and lending professionals who are experts in their field and are genuinely committed to promoting sustainable homeownership to all the consumers they serve, particularly within the growing Hispanic community in the United States . Our members will set the standard for quality service within the real estate and lending industries.

Set forth below is our "Code of Trust" for all NAHREP members. By committing ourselves to conduct all business by the principles in our code, NAHREP members will cultivate the fundamental building block that is needed to rebuild the trust of the consumers and the markets, thereby demonstrating the leadership needed to help all Americans find a way through the current crisis so it is never repeated.

Let us move forward together, confront the problems, find solutions and demonstrate that the Hispanic real estate professional community in the United States is prepared to work tirelessly to resolve this crisis and enable the American Dream of homeownership to be realized and preserved for generations of Americans to come.

Mortgage Originators
"Code of Trust"

NAHREP Believes in Ethical & Responsible Lending

To ensure that real estate professionals promote responsible lending, NAHREP supports the following principles as minimum standards for "NAHREP Code of Trust Certified Professionals" serving Hispanic customers:

- NAHREP Code of Trust Certified Professionals will apply a "prime loan filter" to ensure that consumers, who qualify for a prime loan, are offered a prime loan.

- NAHREP Code of Trust Certified Professionals will only recommend lending products when the ability to repay is made clear by the consumer's credit, assets and financial literacy that enable sustainable homeownership.

- NAHREP Code of Trust Certified Professionals will review each refinance customer's credit profile and apply a net benefit test to prevent equity stripping, and ensure that any loans proposed will provide a demonstrable net benefit to the consumer.

- The Federal Housing Administration (FHA) qualifies loans at the start rate to enable greater customer choice. NAHREP believes this is a sound underwriting principle when adjustment caps are included to limit payment shock. NAHREP endorses that t he fully indexed / fully amortized payment should apply when qualifying for a loan where the margin added to the base rates are at 3.5% or higher and the loan adjustment fixed period is less than 5 years.

- NAHREP Code of Trust Certified Professionals believe consumers are better served when they have escrow accounts, especially when their Combined Loan to Value exceeds 80% Therefore, they will require that lenders provide escrow option s for all mortgage loans. If consumers choose to decline, they will still receive information on the possible consequences of foregoing an escrow. Information provided must include all fees and taxes associated with the transaction.

- NAHREP Code of Trust Certified Professionals will educate consumers about the potentially harmful outcomes of products with "negative amortization". Loan products with negative amortization will not be recommended for first time homebuyers. All customer options will be fully disclosed by the NAHREP certified professional.

- NAHREP Code of Trust Certified Professionals will offer prepayment options only to the extent they provide a demonstrable net savings to the customer by lowering their interest rate. All customer options will be fully disclosed by the NAHREP certified professional, who will ensure the period during which prepayment options apply do not exceed the initial reset period. Consumers should be provided the option of a reasonable period of time to refinance their loans without penalty Borrowers should be provided a disclosure within the time of the Good Faith Estimate that would show what their rate and points would have been if they had chosen an option with No-Prepayment Penalty.

- NAHREP Code of Trust Certified Professionals will ***not*** support or recommend Single Premium Credit Life or Disability Insurance.

NAHREP Believes in Protecting Consumer Choice

In order to protect consumer choice and ensure that consumers can make educated, fully informed decisions about their home loan, NAHREP Code of Trust Certified Professionals are committed to providing the following:

- A simple, bi-lingual information guide to educate consumers on basic choices in lending products available to borrowers.
- Available loan alternatives and how they affect the borrower's rate and terms before determining their final product choice.
- A list of lenders that adhere to the "NAHREP Code of Trust."

NAHREP Believes in Full Disclosure

Full disclosure is an important part of helping consumers make the right decision. NAHREP Code of Trust Certified Professionals w ill ensure the following disclosure steps to ensure that consumers can make informed decisions when it comes to their loans:

- Consumers receive all relevant information

they need to make the right choice for their loan.

- Consumers should receive a guarantee that the final cost/fees could not exceed more than a "reasonable" percent (10%) over the original "Good Faith Estimate and Truth In Lending disclosures " unless there is a change in fees imposed by government agencies (originators cannot control increased recording fees or intangible taxes or documentary stamps) The only exceptions would be if a borrower requested to pay discount points to reduce their rate or pay points to waive the escrow or prepayment penalty period.

- NAHREP believes in a level playing field for all originators. All originators should be required to disclose *all* fees and consumer choices within the good faith estimate time period. In the "Good Faith Estimate and Truth in Lending disclosures," mortgage originators should reflect all fees and charges in the loan. There should be a second disclosure at time of "lock -in" which clearly shows the change in rates if any (based on the Freddie Mac weekly average mortgage rate index) from the initial "Truth in Lending and Good Faith Estimate disclosures."

- NAHREP requires members to fully disclose Affiliated Business Arrangements.

- Where available, Federal documents and disclosures should be available in Spanish upon request. Also where available, state and local documents and disclosures should be provided.

NAHREP Believes in Accountability

Accountability is important for our customers and our industry NAHREP Code of Trust Certified Professionals support the following steps to ensure accountability in our industry:

- NAHREP strongly endorses all mortgage originators be licensed, ensuring enforcement by the appropriate state or federal regulatory entities. All real estate professionals must comply with applicable state and local licensing, and submit to legal background checks.

- FHA approved brokers cannot simultaneously exercise lending and real estate sales functions in the same transaction to protect against inherent conflicts of interest for the consumer. NAHREP Code of Trust Certified Professionals endorse this concept, and commit to implementing an "arms length firewall" in cases where the organization is engaged in multiple business functions.

- Require all real estate professionals have a thorough understanding of applicable state and federal laws —including marketing and privacy laws.

- Lender and origination fee s should be capped and reviewed to maintain pricing that is competitive in the marketplace and reflective of the buyer's financial qualifications.

NAHREP Code of Trust Certified Professional

Real Estate Licensees and Realtors
"Code of Trust"

Obligation to Protect the Consumer

NAHREP Certified Professional Real Estate Licensees and Realtors are committed to protecting and promoting the financial interests of their customers in all aspects of the real estate sales process. Their obligation to serve their customers is their first priority. Equally important is an obligation to treat all parties in the real estate transaction with honesty and respect. When selling or purchasing a home:

- NAHREP Certified Professional Real Estate Licensees and Realtors pledge to protect and promote the financial interest of their client above their own personal financial interest. We will do this by recommending sources of homeownership education when necessary, providing educational materials on the lending process in English and Spanish, and to address all aspects of the transaction honestly and to best interest of the client.

- NAHREP Certified Professional Real Estate Licensees and Realtors will ensure that properties being purchased by Latino consumers meet the customer's stated "intended use" related to the properties zoning and other regulations required by law.

- NAHREP Certified Professional Real Estate Licensees and Realtors will ensure Latino consumers fully understand their rights as it relates to appropriate property inspections, what they should anticipate in a professional appraisal and other factors they should expect from these professional services before the contingency period has been exhausted.

- NAHREP Certified Professional Real Estate Licensees and Realtors will ensure Latino consumers understand their option to purchase a "Homeowners Warranty" protecting them from the risk of unforeseen home maintenance problems that could arise. The limits of coverage, timeframes the policy will apply and all other appropriate information will be included.

NAHREP Believes in Professional and Responsible Service Quality

To ensure that real estate professionals promote responsible lending, NAHREP supports the following principles as minimum standards for NAHREP Certified Professional Real Estate Licensees and Realtors serving Hispanic customers:

- NAHREP Certified Professional Real Estate Licensees and Realtors will consult with each customer to determine their individual housing needs, and ensure that proposed properties meet that consumer's individual need.

- NAHREP Certified Professional Real Estate Licensees and Realtors will make a "good faith effort" to recommend homes for purchase only where the ability to repay is made clear by the consumer.

NAHREP Believes in Protecting Consumer Choice

In order to protect consumer choice and ensure that consumers can make educated, fully informed decisions about their home loan, NAHREP Certified Professional Real Estate Licensees and Realtors are committed to providing the following:

- A simple, bi-lingual information guide to educate consumers on basic choices in lending products available to borrowers.

- Available loan alternatives and how they

affect the borrower's rate and terms.

- A list of lenders that adhere to the "NAHREP Code of Trust."

NAHREP Believes in Full Disclosure

Full disclosures are important parts in helping consumers make the right decision NAHREP Certified Professional Real Estate Licensees and Realtors will ensure the following informational disclosures to en sure that consumers can make informed decisions when it comes to selling or purchasing a home:

- Consumers receive all relevant information including comparable home prices, and any known potential risks such as, but not limited to, flood, zoning, lead pain t, asbestos or any other applicable disclosures necessary to make the right home choice for their personal and financial needs.

- NAHREP Certified Professional Real Estate Licensees and Realtors pledge to honor the letter *and the intended spirit* of the Rea l Estate Services Procedures Act (RESPA) to provide full and forthright disclosure of *any* financial relationships with *any* 3rd party where the customer is paying the fee.

- NAHREP Certified Professional Real Estate Licensees and Realtors should be required to disclose customer choices such as title and insurance with enough time for the consumer to exercise that choice realistically. These must comply within the regulatory and customary practices applicable in their state or region. The timeframe should generally occur during the contingency period of their purchase contract.

- NAHREP Certified Professional Real Estate Licensees and Realtors will fully disclose all Affiliated Business Arrangements that may or may not result in compensation of any sort being paid to the Realtor or Real Estate brokerage.

- When available, federal documents and disclosures should be provided in Spanish upon request. Any additional state and local documents and disclosures should be provided at the customer's request as available.

NAHREP Believes in Accountability

Accountability is important for our customers and our industry. NAHREP Certified Professional Real Estate Licensees and Realtors support the following steps to ensure accountability in our industry:

- NAHREP strongly endorses all Professional Real Estate Licensees and Realtors be licensed in the state or jurisdiction where they do business, ensuring appropriate enforcement by state regulatory entities for all Real Estate Licensees and Realtors.

- FHA -approved mortgage brokers cannot simultaneously exercise lending and real estate sales functions in the same transaction to protect against inherent conflicts of interest for the consumer. NAHREP Certified Professional Real Estate Licensees and Realtors endorse this concept and commit to implementing an "arms length firewall" in cases where their personal organization is engaged in multiple business functions.

- All NAHREP Certified Professional Real Estate Licensees and Realtors commit to having a thorough understanding of applicable state and federal laws - including marketing and privacy laws.

NAHREP Code of Trust Certified Professional

Title, Escrow, Home Inspection and other Loan Closing Services

"Code of Trust"

NAHREP Believes in Full Disclosure

Full disclosures are important parts of helping consumers make the right decision. NAHREP Code of Trust Certified Professionals will ensure the following disclosure steps to ensure that consumers can make informed decisions when it comes to their loans:

- Consumers receive all relevant information they need to make the right choice for their loan and closing service products and service alternatives available to them, and how they affect their rate and terms before determining their final product choices.

- NAHREP Certified Professional s will ensure Latino consumers fully understand their rights as they relate to appropriate property inspections, what they should anticipate in a professional appraisal, and other factors they should expect from these professional services before the contingency period has been exhausted.

- Consumers should receive a guarantee that the final cost/fees could not exceed more than a "reasonable" percent (10%) over the original "Good Faith Estimate and Truth In Lending disclosures " unless there is a change in fees imposed by government agencies (originators cannot control increased recording fees or intangible taxes or documentary stamps) The only exceptions would be if a borrower requested to pay discount points to reduce their rate or pay points to waive the escrow or prepayment penalty period.

- NAHREP believes in a level playing field for all real estate professionals. All real estate professionals should be required to disclose *all* fees and consumer choices within the good faith estimate time period. In the "Good Faith Estimate and Truth in Lending disclosures," real estate professionals should reflect all fees and charges in the loan. There should be a second disclosure at time of "lock - in" which clearly shows the change in rates if any (based on the Freddie Mac weekly average mortgage rate index) from the initial "Truth in Lending and Good Faith Estimate disclosures."

- NAHREP requires members to fully disclose Affiliated Business Arrangements.

- Where available, Federal documents and disclosures should be available in Spanish upon request. Also where available, state and local documents and disclosures should be provided in Spanish upon request.

- Require all real estate professionals have a thorough understanding of applicable state and federal laws —including marketing and privacy laws.

NAHREP Believes in Protecting Consumer Choice

In order to protect consumer choice and ensure that consumers can make educated, fully informed decisions about their home loan, NAHREP Code of Trust Certified Professionals are committed to providing the following:

- A simple, bi -lingual information guide to educate consumers on basic choices in lending and closing service products and services should be available to borrowers.

- Borrowers will be made aware of available

loan and closing service products and service alternatives available to them, and how they affect their rate and terms before determining their final product choices.

- NAHREP will make available a list of lenders that adhere to the "NAHREP Code of Trust."

Appraisals

- NAHREP 'Code of Trust' Certified Professionals will comply with FIRREA and USPAP policies for appraisals. These policies dictate only state licensed or certified appraisers will be used to perform appraisals NAHREP also stipulates that no one with a financial interest in the transaction may order or influence the selection of the appraiser, or attempt to influence the property valuation NAHREP Code of Trust Certified Professionals should make access available to he published USPAP guidelines.

- NAHREP 'Code of Trust' Certified Professionals should ensure that its consumers fully understand their rights as it relates to appropriate property inspections, what they should anticipate in a professional appraisal and other factors they should expect from these professional services.

- NAHREP 'Code of Trust' Certified Professionals will advise customers that n o one with a financial interest in the transaction may order or influence the ordering of an appraisal or the selection of the appraiser.

Closing Services

- NAHREP Code of Trust Certified Professionals believe consumers are better served when they have escrow accounts, especially when their Combined Loan to Value exceeds 80% Therefore, they will require lenders provide escrow options for all mortgage loans If consumers choose to decline, they will still receive information on the possible consequences of foregoing an escrow. Information provided must include all fees and taxes associated with the transaction.

- NAHREP Code of Trust Certified Professionals will ***not*** support or recommend Single Premium Credit Life or Disability Insurance.

- NAHREP Certified Professional s will ensure Latino consumers fully understand their rights as they relate to appropriate property inspections, what they should anticipate in a professional appraisal, and other factors they should expect from these professional services before the contingency period has been exhausted.

- NAHREP Code of Trust Certified Professionals will ensure Latino consumers understand their option to purchase a "Homeowners Warranty" protecting them from the risk of unforeseen home maintenance problems that could arise. The limits of coverage, timeframes the policy will apply and all other appropriate information will be included.

NAHREP Supports Community-Based Counseling and Regulatory Enforcement

- Working with the Conference of State Bank Regulators NAHREP Certified Professional s support the establishment of a "whistle blower hotline" for industry professionals and consumers to report allegations of misconduct or warn authorities about predatory lenders and practitioners. An industry based "peer review with due process" including the opportunity for response from individuals reported to the hotline is recommended.

- NAHREP Certified Professional support partner ships with counseling providers to educate borrowers on homeownership for consumers in need of assistance during the lending process.

- NAHREP Certified Professional s support the establishment of a borrowers' hotline to provide counseling and support services for consumers in need of assistance when they are at risk of default or foreclosure, and are committed to counseling customers to "call their lender" as soon as possible when they are faced with the potential of payment default.

Builders

- NAHREP believes in a level playing field amongst lenders and closing agents. Currently, on transactions where there is a builder involved who is offering financing through a "preferred lender", there is little or no protection for the borrower Borrowers should be provided with a fully completed

HUD 1 & 2 from the "preferred closing agent" no later than 30 days prior to the expected closing date This should include an option to lock the loan in at the rate and price quoted for this pre -closing statement The lock period should be for 60 days to allow for any unexpected delay in the closing .In this manner, the borrower can fully and completely assess if the "preferred financing" will be a benefit or if the borrower would be better served by closing through a different broker and/or title agent.

About the Authors

Sylvia A. Alvarez & Walter Walker, Jr.

A native of Cuba raised in Tampa, Florida, Sylvia A. Alvarez, Co-Author of *American Nightmare,* has an impressive background of experience and leadership in the affordable housing industry. One of her greatest achievements has been co-founding the Housing and Education Alliance (HEA). This HUD-certified housing consultant agency provides First Time Homebuyer Education Classes, One-on-One Housing Counseling, Foreclosure Prevention Consulting Services and serves as an Affordable Housing Developer. With her guidance, since its inception in 2002, HEA has earned its distinction as a leading housing services provider on Florida's West Coast, vividly reflected by the distinguished recognition the agency has received. This distinction has included receiving the Tampa Housing Authority's "Housing Hero Award," Catholic Charities' "Outstanding Community Services Award" and the Tampa Bay Hispanic Chamber of Commerce's "Non-Profit of the Year Award." Ms. Alvarez is a two-term member of Hillsborough County's Affordable Housing Task Force and has been a licensed realtor for more than twenty years. With negative changes taking place in the housing market, the demand for HEA services eventually became so great she realized she needed to find another way to reach more people facing foreclosure – not just in the Tampa Bay area, but throughout the country. The answer she came up with was co-writing a book to give people information, referral sources, options and hope. That book is *American Nightmare.*

For more than a decade *American Nightmare* Co-Author Walter Walker, Jr. has been involved in the affordable housing industry after a long, distinguished career in the U.S. Navy, followed by years in the private sector in various capacities. These have included: positions related to sales and training for various companies; operating his own HR/personal dynamics firm; and both teaching and serving as a contract instructor and facilitator for community colleges. His extensive housing background includes working for RTC (Resolution Trust Corporation), the Alliance for Affordable, Housing, Inc. and presently Housing and Education Alliance in Tampa, Florida. The true depth of his knowledge, passion and experience in home ownership counseling can be seen in these statistics: *Over the years he has taught, either personally or in a team environment, 20,000-plus people the process of buying and keeping their first home – 5,000 of whom ultimately made their dream a reality*. A licensed Realtor® as well as a housing and credit counselor, Mr. Walker also provides counseling in terms of helping people who need pre-purchase advice and credit "repair." Although he has assisted many people with understanding what is required to keep and maintain their home, there are countless others he would like to help. Hence, he looks at his co-authorship of the *American Nightmare* as part of the solution to reaching those individuals he has been unable to help personally, but who truly need professional guidance to protect their homes from becoming another foreclosure statistic.

The authors are available for speaking engagements and group training. To schedule, call the Housing & Education Alliance, Inc. at:

813-261-5151